U0085054

一本屬於全家人的……

HOME
ENGLISH

家庭英語

By Daisie M.T. Chen/Thomas Deneau

編者的話

如果學英語像學國語一樣容易……

這是學英族的共同心願。「家庭英語」（*Home English*）編輯的目的，就在幫助讀者創造類似母語的語言學習環境；它將日常生活中的點點滴滴，都化成學英語的素材，教讀者利用與家人相處的時光，充實彼此的英語能力！

全書內容的編排，是以家中不同場所為背景，如客廳（*the living room*）、臥房（*the bedroom*）、廚房（*the kitchen*）、浴室（*the bathroom*）等，共分十三單元。每單元先有**圖解單字**，圖示家中細部結構，中英對照，一目了然；**Warm-Up 暖身單字**，讓您掌握各種家庭活動的必備單字；**實用例句**網羅家庭生活中，天天都用得到的句子，簡單易學。**會話範例**依不同場景，將實用例句擴大成完整對話，內容輕鬆有趣。

此外，為順應環保潮流，本書特別收錄許多**家庭小常識**，教您有效節約能源、廢物利用，讓您學會英語、增長生活常識，同時又能為環保盡一份心力，一舉數得！

「家庭英語」的確是您在家中輕鬆學英語的好幫手，它實用的題材，體貼的編排，讓您一學就會。您會發現，原來學英語真的可以像學國語一樣容易！

編者　謹識

CONTENTS

UNIT ▶ 11

Visitors
訪 客

UNIT ▶ 12

Illness
生 病

UNIT ▶ 13

Small Talk
閒話家常

Unit 1

The Living Room 客廳

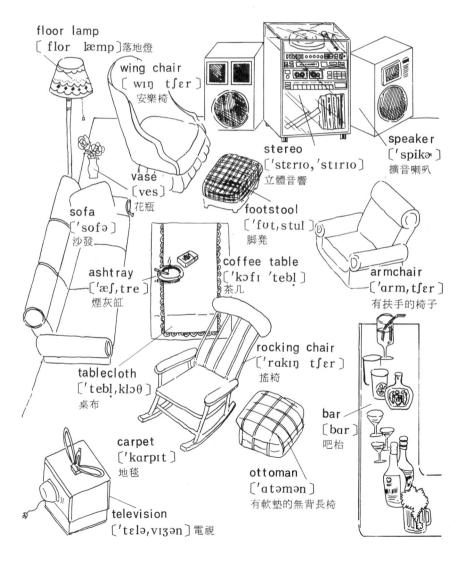

floor lamp
〔flor læmp〕落地燈

wing chair
〔wɪŋ tʃɛr〕
安樂椅

stereo
〔'stɛrɪo,'stɪrɪo〕
立體音響

speaker
〔'spikɚ〕
擴音喇叭

vase
〔ves〕
花瓶

sofa
〔'sofə〕
沙發

footstool
〔'fʊt,stul〕
脚凳

ashtray
〔'æʃ,tre〕
煙灰缸

coffee table
〔'kɔfɪ 'tebl〕
茶几

armchair
〔'arm,tʃɛr〕
有扶手的椅子

rocking chair
〔'rakɪŋ tʃɛr〕
搖椅

tablecloth
〔'tebl,klɔθ〕
桌布

bar
〔bar〕
吧枱

carpet
〔'karpɪt〕
地毯

ottoman
〔'atəmən〕
有軟墊的無背長椅

television
〔'tɛlə,vɪʒən〕電視

Warm-up

stereo〔'stɛrɪo , 'stɪrɪo〕*n.* 立體音響
CD player 雷射唱盤　CD 雷射唱片（＝compact disk）
amp〔æmp〕*n.* 擴音器（＝amplifier〔'æmplə,faɪə〕）
tape deck 錄音卡座　　　　radio station 廣播電台
DJ 唱片播放者（＝disc jockey）
commercial〔kə'mɝʃəl〕*n.* 電台廣告
speaker〔'spikə〕*n.* 擴音喇叭
record〔rɪ'kɔrd〕*v.* 將～錄音；拷貝（卡帶）
headphones〔'hɛd,fonz〕*n.pl.* 雙耳式耳機
ICRT(International Community Radio Taipei)台北國際社區電台
loud〔laʊd〕*adj.* 大聲的　　　turn off 關掉
popular song 流行歌曲　　　record player 電唱機

●　聽音響　●

♤ Will you turn the volume down? I'm trying to sleep!

你能不能關小聲一點？我正想睡覺。

♤ Does your **stereo** have a **CD player**?

你的音響有 CD 唱盤嗎？

♤ How many **amps** is your stereo?

你的音響有幾個喇叭？

♤ This stereo has a **tape deck** and a CD player.

這套音響有一個錄音卡座和一組 CD 唱盤。

♤ What **radio station** do you like?

你喜歡哪一個電台？

♤ I don't like to listen to that **DJ**. He's boring.

我不喜歡聽那個ＤＪ說話，他很無趣。

♤ Do you have the new **CD**? I just bought it yesterday.

你有這片新ＣＤ嗎？我昨天才買的。

♤ Can I borrow your CD for a couple days?

我可不可以借你的ＣＤ聽幾天？

♤ If I play the stereo too **loud**, the neighbors will complain.

如果我音響開太大聲，鄰居會抱怨。

♤ **Turn off** that stereo and study right now!

把音響關掉，馬上去念書。

♤ What kind of **speakers** do you have?

你的擴音喇叭是哪一型？

♤ Can your CD player **record** other CDs?

你的ＣＤ唱盤可拷貝其他的ＣＤ嗎？

**

a couple (of) 幾個　　complain〔kəmˈplen〕*v.* 抱怨

Listening to the Stereo·····················

A： ***If I play the stereo too loud, the neighbors will complain***.
如果我音響開太大聲，鄰居會抱怨。

B： My neighbor complains too. He's such a grouch.
我的鄰居也會抱怨，他脾氣很不好。　　＊ grouch〔graʊtʃ〕*n.* 不高興的人

A： That's why now I listen to my headphones late at night.
所以現在深夜我都用耳機聽。

B： Hey, that's not a bad idea！ I'll have to get my own
headphones. 嘿，這主意不錯喔！我也要去買副耳機。

　　　　　　＊　　　　　＊　　　　　＊

A： I like to listen to ICRT. ***What radio station do you like***？
我喜歡聽ICRT，你喜歡聽哪個電台？

B： I like WXYZ. They don't have as many commercials.
我喜歡WXYZ，他們比較少插播廣告。

A： That's true, but they don't play the most popular songs as
often. 那倒是真的，不過他們較不常播流行歌曲。

B： Well, actually I like to listen to old songs.
嗯，事實上我喜歡聽老歌。

　　　　　　＊　　　　　＊　　　　　＊

A： ***This stereo has a tape deck and a CD player***.
這套音響有一個錄音卡座和一組CD唱盤。

B： Does it have a record player？ 有唱片唱盤嗎？

A： No, I didn't want one because I like the sound of CDs
better. 沒有，我不想要因為我較喜歡CD的聲音。

B： I still listen to records sometimes.
我有時還聽聽唱片。

Warm-up

show〔ʃo〕*n.* 表演；節目   change〔tʃendʒ〕*v.* 轉（台）

channel〔'tʃænl〕*n.* 頻道

newscaster〔'njuz,kæstɚ, -,kɑstɚ〕*n.* 主播；播報員

actor〔'æktɚ〕*n.* 演員   turn off 關掉

news program 新聞節目

sitcom〔'sɪtkəm〕*n.* 單元喜劇

talk show 脫口秀   turn on 打開

switch〔swɪtʃ〕*v.* 轉換（台）   switch off 關掉

documentary〔,dɑkjə'mɛntərɪ〕*n.* 紀錄影片

NHK（Japan Broadcasting Corporation）日本傳播公司

favorite〔'fevərɪt〕*adj.* 最喜愛的

series〔'sɪriz, 'sɪrɪz〕*n.pl.* 單元劇

scream〔skrim〕*n.* 可笑的情節

dull〔dʌl〕*adj.* 單調的   silly〔'sɪlɪ〕*adj.* 愚蠢的

childish〔'tʃaɪldɪʃ〕*adj.* 幼稚的

remote control 遙控器   record〔rɪ'kɔrd〕*v.* 錄

VCR（video cassette recorder）錄放影機

tube〔tjub〕*n.* 電視頻道   nightly news 夜間新聞

commercial〔kə'mɝʃəl〕*n.* 商業廣告

scene〔sin〕*n.* 一幕；一場

dubbed-in〔'dʌbd,ɪn〕*adj.* 配音的

schedule〔'skɛdʒʊl〕*v.* 排定時間

murder mystery 殺人謎案   serial〔'sɪrɪəl〕*n.* 連續劇

newscast〔'njuz,kæst, -,kɑst〕*n.* 新聞報導

game show 益智節目   variety show 綜藝節目

comedy〔'kɑmədɪ〕*n.* 喜劇   sports news 體育新聞

mute〔mjut〕*v.* 消音   screen〔skrin〕*n.* 電視螢光幕

soap opera 通俗的電視連續劇；肥皂劇（因最初由肥皂公司提
  供而得名）

────────● 看電視 ●────────

♤ Do you want to watch TV? 你要看電視嗎？

♤ What a boring / an interesting *show*! 這節目眞無聊 / 有趣 。

♤ Please *change* the *channel*. 請轉台 。

♤ Watching a baseball game is so exciting. 看棒球賽好刺激 。

♤ That woman *newscaster* is really pretty. 那個女主播的確很漂亮 。

♤ I don't like that *actor*. He's such a snob. 我不喜歡那個演員，他眞是勢利 。

♤ What channel do you want to watch? 你要看哪一台？

♤ Can you *turn off* the TV for a minute? 你能不能把電視關掉一會兒？

♤ I think that *news* program is educational. 我認爲那個新聞性節目富有教育意義 。

♤ Can I *turn on* the TV? 我可以開電視嗎？

✱✱────────────────

snob〔snɑb〕*n.* 勢利小人

♤ Actually, I prefer to watch *sitcoms*.

事實上，我比較喜歡看單元喜劇。

♤ That *talk show* is really funny.

那個脫口秀節目實在很好笑。

♤ What are you watching on TV?

你在看什麼節目？

♤ I want to watch the football game on Channel 3.

我想看第三台轉播的足球賽。

♤ *Switch off* the television when you leave.

你離開時，要把電視關掉。

♤ There's a *documentary* on *NHK*.

NHK 電台在播紀錄片。

♤ Today is Wednesday, so my *favorite series* will be on.

今天是星期三，所以將有我最愛看的單元劇。

♤ This comedy is a *scream*.

這齣喜劇很好笑。

♤ It's *dull* / *silly* / *childish*.

真無聊／真笨／真幼稚。

♤ Please pass me the *remote control*.

請把遙控器遞給我。

♤ I *recorded* a program on my *VCR*.

我用錄影機錄下了一個節目。

♤ I wonder what's on the *tube* tonight.

我不知道今晚電視有什麼節目。

♤ I won't go to bed until I finish watching the *nightly news*.

我要看完夜間新聞再去睡。

♤ I'll go to the bathroom when the next *commercial* comes on.

下一個廣告出現時，我就要去上廁所。

♤ I don't understand why they cut such an important *scene*.

眞搞不懂他們爲何把這麼重要的畫面刪去。

♤ I can't stand these *dubbed-in* voices.

我受不了這些配過音的對話。

♤ Why do they *schedule* good shows at such inconvenient times?

他們爲何把好的節目安排在這麼差的時段播出？

♤ This guy's on TV all the time lately.

最近這個人在電視上頻頻露臉。

♤ Do you really have to watch these *reruns*? You've seen them all months ago!

你眞的非得看這些重播嗎？幾個月前你全都看過了！

＊＊

rerun〔'ri,rʌn〕 *n.* 重播

家庭小常識　電冰箱、電視機要放置在乾燥而涼爽的地方，最好是距離放置的牆壁大約三十公分以上，使傳熱能迅速擴散，這樣電冰箱、電視機可延年益壽哦！

Watching TV

A : **Can I turn on the TV?** 我可以打開電視嗎？

B : Not until you finish your homework. 做完功課才可以。

A : But mom, my favorite show is on right now.
   但是媽，我最喜歡的節目現在正在播出。

B : Then do your homework right now and you can watch it.
   那麼，你立刻做功課就可以看了。

*   *   *

A : I like to watch murder mysteries.
   我喜歡看謀殺謎案偵探片。

B : **Actually, I prefer to watch sitcoms.**
   事實上，我比較喜歡單元喜劇。

A : Well, either one is better than watching a soap opera.
   嗯，不管哪一種都比肥皂劇好看。

B : I agree. 我同意。

*   *   *

A : **What are you watching on TV**, Judy?
   茱蒂，妳在看什麼電視節目？

B : It's "Miami Vice", a police story. What kind of TV
   shows do you like?
   「邁阿密風雲」，是一部警匪片。你喜歡哪種電視節目？

A : I'm interested in talk shows, but most of them are too
   difficult for me to understand.
   我喜歡脫口秀，但這種節目大多很難聽懂。

B : Are they? I don't like talk shows very much.
   是嗎？我不是很喜歡脫口秀。

Warm-up

empty〔'ɛmptɪ〕v. 倒空	remove〔rɪ'muv〕v. 掃除
move〔muv〕v. 移動	dust〔dʌst〕v. 拭去灰塵
carpet〔'kɑrpɪt〕n. 地毯	ceiling〔'silɪŋ〕n. 天花板
cleaner〔'klinɚ〕n. 清潔劑	wring out 絞出（水來）
rag〔ræg〕n. 破布	messy〔'mɛsɪ〕adj. 雜亂的
furniture〔'fɝnɪtʃɚ〕n. 家具	get rid of 免除
blind〔blaɪnd〕n. 百葉窗；窗簾	
wastebasket〔'west,bæskɪt〕n. 字紙簍	
vacuum〔'vækjʊəm〕v. 用吸塵器掃除	
straighten〔'stretn̩〕v. 弄正	

● 打 掃 ●

♠ Can you *empty* the *wastebasket*? 你去倒垃圾好嗎？

♠ The ashtrays need to be emptied. 煙灰缸該清理了。

♠ Please *vacuum* the *carpet*. 請用吸塵器吸地毯。

♠ *Dust* the *furniture*. 拭去家具上的灰塵。

♠ Can you *remove* the cobwebs from the *ceiling*? 你可不可以去把天花板上的蜘蛛網清理乾淨？

ashtray〔'æʃ,tre〕n. 煙灰缸　　cobweb〔'kɑb,wɛb〕n. 蜘蛛網

♤ These windows need cleaning. 　　窗子該洗了。

♤ I need someone to dust the ***blinds***. 　　我需要有人去掃掉百葉窗上的灰塵。

♤ Please put these old magazines in the closet. 　　請把這些舊雜誌放到櫃子裏。

♤ We need to buy a ***hat rack***. 　　我們得買一個帽架。

♤ The picture on the wall needs to be ***straightened***. 　　牆上的畫應該找個人來擺正。

♤ Please help me ***move*** the bookcase. 　　請幫我搬走這個書架。

♤ Do we have any glass ***cleaner***? 　　我們有沒有玻璃清潔劑？

♤ Oh! It's so ***messy***. 　　噢，眞是亂七八糟。

♤ I clean the floor with a wet ***rag***. 　　我用濕抹布擦淨地板。

♤ I'll ***wring out*** the rag. 　　我會把抹布擰乾。

** ———————————————

rack〔ræk〕*n.* 架子　　bookcase〔'buk,kes〕*n.* 書架

家庭小常識　用舊報紙擦玻璃窗的效果可比魔術靈、妙管家好用得多了：先把舊報紙浸在水中，吸飽水分，然後輕輕擠成一團，讓水分流出，就可用來擦玻璃，擦過之後，再用乾布擦掉水分，玻璃就能清潔、明亮。

Cleaning Up ···

A : ***Can you remove the cobwebs from the ceiling*** ?
你能否把天花板上的蜘蛛網清掉？

B : But I like spiders. 可是我喜歡蜘蛛。

A : Well I don't. Now get to work. 嗯，我可不喜歡。開始清理吧！

B : But they ***get rid of*** flies and mosquitoes.
但他們能除去蒼蠅、蚊子。

A : I know, but I still don't like spiders.
我知道，不過我還是不喜歡蜘蛛。

*   *   *

A : ***These windows need to be cleaned***. 窗子該洗了。

B : But I just washed them yesterday. 可是我昨天才剛洗過。

A : You know that everyone burns coal around here.
你知道這附近每個人都燃燒生煤。

B : I know, but I still don't like to wash the windows so often. 我曉得，但我還是不喜歡這麼常洗窗子。

*   *   *

A : ***Can you put these magazines in the closet*** ?
你能不能把這些雜誌放到櫥子裡？

B : Which closet ? 哪個櫥子？

A : The one out in the hallway to your left. 你左手邊走道上的那個。

B : Do you keep all your old magazines there ?
你所有的舊雜誌都放在那兒嗎？

**

mosquito 〔məˈskito〕 *n.* 蚊   coal 〔kol〕 *n.* 煤炭
hallway 〔ˈhɔlˌwe〕 *n.* 走廊

Warm-up

chess〔tʃɛs〕*n.* 西洋棋　　　board game 需用棋盤的遊戲

checkers〔'tʃɛkəz〕*n. pl.* 西洋棋　poker〔'pokə〕*n.* 撲克牌

cards〔kɑrdz〕*n. pl.* 紙牌；撲克牌　hide and seek 捉迷藏

play house (兒童)扮家家酒　　deal〔dil〕*v.* 發牌

cheat〔tʃit〕*v.* 作弊；詐欺　　count〔kaʊnt〕*v.* 數

tie〔taɪ〕*n.* 不分勝負　　　Monopoly〔mə'nɑpəlɪ〕*n.* 大富翁

blackjack〔'blæk,dʒæk〕*n.* 二十一點

Mahjong〔mɑ'dʒɔŋ , -'dʒɑŋ〕*n.* 麻將

● 玩遊戲 ●

♤ It takes a long time to learn how to play *chess*.

學會下棋需要很長的時間。

♤ Do you know how to play *Mahjong*?

你知道麻將怎麼打嗎？

♤ Cut the *cards* and *deal*.

切牌，然後發牌。

♤ Playing *checkers* is easier than chess.

下西洋棋比下象棋簡單。

♤ Don't *cheat* at cards.

玩牌別作弊。

♤ Have you played *Monopoly* before?

你以前玩過「大富翁」嗎？

♤ In *blackjack* the dealer takes all *ties*.

玩二十一點時，不分勝負則算莊家贏。

♤ We like to play *poker* on weekends.

週末時我們喜歡玩撲克牌。

♤ Let's *play house* !

我們來玩扮家家酒。

♤ We can play *hide and seek*. I'll *count* to one hundred. Ready?

我們可以玩捉迷藏,我要數到一百,準備好了嗎?

♤ He played poker all night last night so I'm afraid he can't come to the phone now.

他昨晚玩了整晚的牌,我想他現在恐怕無法起來接電話。

♤ My uncle spends hours playing chess with his buddies whenever they come over.

我舅舅每次都和他那些來家裏的夥伴們下西洋棋。

---

buddy 〔'bʌdɪ〕 *n.* 夥伴;弟兄

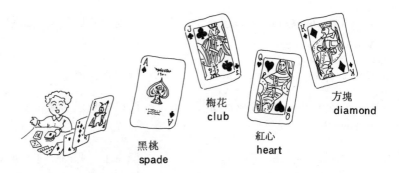

梅花
club

方塊
diamond

黑桃
spade

紅心
heart

Playing Games ···

A : ***Do you know how to play Mahjong*?**
你知道麻將怎麼打嗎？

B : No. My parents play it a lot but I don't.
不知道，我爸媽常打，可是我不會。

A : It's easy. I'll teach you how to play.
那很簡單，我來教你。

      *   *   *

A : ***Have you played Monopoly before*?**
你以前玩過大富翁嗎？

B : No. What kind of game is it?
沒有，那是什麼遊戲？

A : It's a ***board game***. You try to buy up all the land so you can increase the rent.
一種棋盤遊戲。你盡可能的買下所有土地，好讓租金增加。

B : Sounds just like a land speculator.
聽起來好像炒地皮的遊戲。

A : You got it. Let's play a game.
沒錯，我們來玩吧！

**────────────────────

speculator〔'spɛkjəˌletə〕*n*. 商場郎中；投機者

Warm-up

beer〔bɪr〕*n.* 啤酒	gin and tonic 琴酒加蘇打水
martini〔mɑr'tinɪ〕*n.* 馬丁尼酒	scotch and soda 威士忌蘇打
whisky〔'hwɪskɪ〕*n.* 威士忌	coffee〔'kɔfɪ〕*n.* 咖啡
soda〔'sodə〕*n.* 蘇打水	drink〔drɪŋk〕*n.* 飲料
ice cube 冰塊	on the rocks 加冰塊的
fix〔fɪks〕*v.* 調製	pint〔paɪnt〕*n.* 品脫(容積單位)
stout〔staʊt〕*n.* 濃烈的黑啤酒	shake〔ʃek〕*v.* 搖動
stir〔stɝ〕*v.* 攪拌	bitter〔'bɪtə〕*n.* 苦啤酒
lager〔'lɑgə〕*n.* 拉格啤酒	

——————●在吧枱 ●——————

♤ What would you like to drink?　　你想喝什麼?

♤ I'd like an orange *soda*.　　我想要一杯橘子汽水。

♤ Do you have any cold *beer*?　　你有沒有冰啤酒?

♤ I'll have a *gin and tonic* /
　 a martini.　　我要一杯琴酒加蘇打水／一杯馬丁尼。

♤ I'll make you an Irish *coffee*.　　我替你泡一杯愛爾蘭咖啡。

♤ Can you add a few *ice cubes*
　 to my *drink*?　　你能不能在我的飲料裏加些冰塊?

**———————————————

　 Irish〔'aɪrɪʃ〕*adj.* 愛爾蘭的　　add〔æd〕*v.* 加

♤ Would you like a ***scotch and soda***?

你想喝杯威士忌蘇打嗎？

♤ ***Whisky on the rocks***, please.

請給我一杯加冰塊的威士忌。

♤ What do you have in the bar?

你的酒吧裏有什麼飲料？

♤ Can you ***fix*** me a drink?

能不能為我調杯飲料？

♤ Would you like something cold to drink?

你想喝點冷飲嗎？

♤ Don't you think you're drinking too fast?

你不認為自己喝得太快了嗎？

♤ I'd like a ***pint*** of ***lager***, please.

請給我一品脫拉格啤酒。

♤ What a day! I need a drink!

今天真是忙壞了！我要喝杯飲料！

♤ Long time no see! Come on in and have a beer.

好久不見！請進來喝杯啤酒吧！

家庭小常識　大家都知道酒喝多害人害己，但酒也可以救人，這你可能不知道！如遭水溺、受寒凍、自縊者，若一息尚存，以溫酒少許灌飲，或能起死回生。至於久病有虛脫跡象的人，則可用酒半匙和溫水飲用；因跌打而損傷的，可用酒與水各半洗傷處。

At the Bar ....

A: What a day! I need a drink! ***What do you have in the bar***? 今天眞是忙壞了！我要喝杯飲料！你的酒吧裏有什麼？

B: Just about anything you feel like drinking, buddy.
你想喝的大槪都有，老兄。

A: Good! I'll have a gin and tonic.
好極了！我要一杯琴酒加蘇打水。

*　　　　　*　　　　　*

A: ***Do you have any cold beer***? 你有沒有冰啤酒？

B: Sure! I keep all kinds of beer. Which one do you like?
當然！我有各種啤酒，你喜歡哪一種？

A: I'd like a pint of lager, please.
請給我一品脫拉格啤酒。

*　　　　　*　　　　　*

A: I'm beat! Can you fix me a drink?
我累死了！能不能爲我調杯飲料？

B: Sure! What do you want? 當然可以，你要喝什麼？

A: I'll have a martini. And ***can you please add a few ice cubes to my drink***?
我要一杯馬丁尼。還有，能不能在飲料裏加些冰塊？

B: No problem! 沒問題！

Unit 2

The Kitchen 厨房

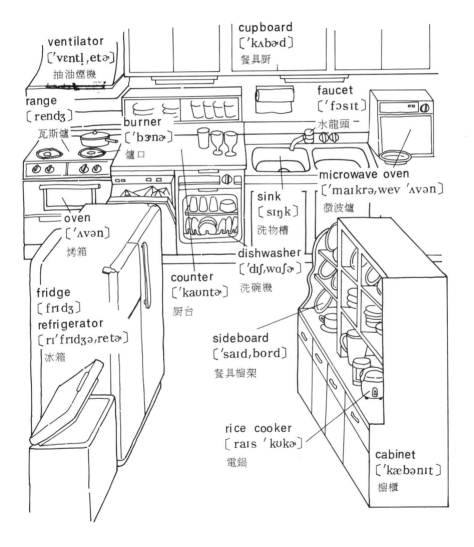

ventilator
['vɛntḷˌetə]
抽油煙機

cupboard
['kʌbəd]
餐具厨

range
[rendʒ]
瓦斯爐

burner
['bɜnə]
爐口

faucet
['fɔsɪt]
水龍頭

microwave oven
['maɪkrəˌwev 'ʌvən]
微波爐

oven
['ʌvən]
烤箱

sink
[sɪŋk]
洗物槽

fridge
[frɪdʒ]
refrigerator
[rɪ'frɪdʒəˌretə]
冰箱

counter
['kaʊntə]
厨台

dishwasher
['dɪʃˌwaʃə]
洗碗機

sideboard
['saɪdˌbord]
餐具橱架

rice cooker
[raɪs 'kʊkə]
電鍋

cabinet
['kæbənɪt]
橱櫃

Warm-up

pan〔pæn〕*n*. 鍋子	dish〔dɪʃ〕*n*. 盤碟
soak〔sok〕*v*. 浸	wash〔waʃ〕*v*. 洗
wipe〔waɪp〕*v*. 擦	sweep〔swip〕*v*. 掃
scrub〔skrʌb〕*v*. 洗刷	wax〔wæks〕*v*. 打蠟於
sink〔sɪŋk〕*n*. 水槽	faucet〔'fɔsɪt〕*n*. 水龍頭
broom〔brum〕*n*. 掃把	stopper〔'stɑpɚ〕*n*. 塞子
mop〔mɑp〕*v*. 用拖把擦 *n*. 拖把	
detergent〔dɪ'tɝdʒənt〕*n*. 清潔劑	
dishcloth〔'dɪʃ,klɔθ〕*n*. 抹布	

● 清 掃 ●

♤ ***Soak*** the ***pan*** in water. 　　把鍋子浸在水裏。

♤ ***Wash the dishes*** for me, will you? 　　請幫我洗碗好嗎？

♤ There's some ***detergent*** under the ***sink***. 　　水槽下面有清潔劑。

♤ ***Wipe*** your hands with that ***dishcloth***. 　　你用那塊抹布擦手。

♤ Can you plug the sink with that ***stopper***? 　　用塞子把水槽塞住好嗎？

＊＊

plug〔plʌg〕*v*. 以塞子塞住

♤ Use that dishcloth to dry the dishes.

用那條抹布把碗盤擦乾。

♤ Will you lift the table while I *sweep* the floor?

我在掃地時，你把桌子抬起來好嗎？

♤ Please bring me a *mop*.

請把拖把拿給我。

♤ Would you mind *mopping* the floor?

你能不能拖一下地板？

♤ The trash needs to be taken out.

垃圾該拿出去倒了！

♤ What did you do? The kitchen is a mess.

你做了什麼？整個廚房亂七八糟。

♤ The floor needs to be *scrubbed*.

地板該刷了！

♤ Have you seen the *broom*?

你有沒有看到掃把？

♤ We need to *wax* the floor.

我們該在地板上打蠟了。

＊＊────────────────

lift〔lɪft〕v. 抬起　　trash〔træʃ〕n. 垃圾
mess〔mɛs〕n. 雜亂的一團

Cleaning Up ··

A : ***Would you mind mopping the floor*** ?
　　你能不能拖一下地板？

B : Well, actually I've got to meet my cousin at the airport
　　soon. 嗯，事實上我馬上要去機場接我堂妹。

A : In that case, can you remember to do it tomorrow ?
　　那樣的話，明天你會記得拖嗎？

B : Sure, no problem. 當然，沒問題。

＊　　　　　＊　　　　　＊

A : There's a VIP coming tomorrow. ***We have to wax the***
　　floor. 明天有位貴賓要來，我們必須給地板打打蠟。

B : Another VIP ? That's the third one this week.
　　又來一位貴賓？他是這禮拜第三位了。

A : That's the way it goes. Maybe next week we won't have
　　any. 就是這樣囉，但也許下禮拜一位也沒有。

B : I hope so. 希望如此。

家庭小常識　家庭主婦、主夫們面對焦黑的鍋底，往往感到十分頭大。現在可有對付的妙招了：在使用之前，先用肥皂塗上一層，清洗時就不用再煩惱了。

Warm-up

egg-beater 打蛋器

rolling pin 擀麵棍

sauce〔sɔs〕*n.* 醬；調味汁

chop〔tʃɑp〕*v.* 剁；切

toast〔tost〕*v.* 烤(麵包)

frozen food 冷凍食品

wheat〔hwit〕*n.* 小麥

stir-fry 炒

chopping block 砧板(＝cutting board)

ingredient〔ɪn'gridɪənt〕*n.* 材料

broccoli〔'brɑkəlɪ, 'brɑklɪ〕*n.* 花椰菜

parboil〔'pɑr‚bɔɪl〕*v.* 煮成半熟

warm up 把(變冷的菜餚)重新加熱

melted〔'mɛltɪd〕*adj.* 已融解的

beefsteak〔'bif‚stek〕*n.* 牛排

knife〔naɪf〕*n.* 有柄的小刀

mixing bowl 調配用的碗

masher〔'mæʃɚ〕*n.* 搗碎機

powder〔'paudɚ〕*n.* 粉

dip〔dɪp〕*v.* 沾

serve〔sɝv〕*v.* 上(菜)

flavor〔'flevɚ〕*n.* 味道

slice〔slaɪs〕*v.* 切薄片　*n.* 薄片

broil〔brɔɪl〕*v.* 烤

●────────── ● 準備餐點 ● ──────────

♤ I need to buy a bigger ***mixing bowl***.

我必須去買一個大一點的調配用碗。

♤ Do you know how to use a ***rolling pin***?

你知道怎麼用擀麵棍嗎？

♤ Can you ***chop up*** some carrots?

你可不可以剁碎一些紅蘿蔔？

♤ Rinse the ***chopping block*** before you use it.

用砧板前要先沖洗。

♤ Use that *egg-beater* to mix the *ingredients*.　用打蛋器混合這些材料。

♤ You're supposed to *dip* fritters in *sauce*.　你應該把油炸餅沾醬吃。

♤ Can you pass that potato *masher* over to me?　能不能把馬鈴薯搗碎機遞給我？

♤ Fill the kettle with water.　把茶壺裝滿水。

♤ Do you like brown rice or white rice?　你喜歡糙米還是白米？

♤ *Parboil* the *broccoli* and *serve* with *melted* butter.　把花椰菜煮半熟，然後加上融化的奶油。

♤ Put some garlic *powder* on that French bread.　在法國麵包上灑點大蒜粉。

♤ You can help me *toast* some bread.　你可以幫我烤麵包。

♤ Do you know the ingredients for sponge cake?　你知道做海綿蛋糕的原料是什麼嗎？

♤ When I'm tired I usually serve them *frozen food*.　我很累的時候，通常弄冷凍食物給他們吃。

----

rinse〔rɪns〕*v.* 沖洗　　mix〔mɪks〕*v.* 混合　　fritter〔'frɪtɚ〕*n.* 油炸餅
brown rice 糙米　　garlic〔'gɑrlɪk〕*n.* 大蒜　　sponge〔spʌndʒ〕*n.* 海綿

♤ I'll just **warm up** the leftovers.

我只要把剩菜熱一熱。

♤ Maybe I'll have **beefsteak** for
a change.

也許我會做牛排來換換口味。

♤ I'll chop some vegetables and
stir-fry them.

我要切些青菜來炒。

♤ I'll **broil** a fish.

我要烤一條魚。

♤ Put the food on a plate.

把食物放在盤子中。

♤ Be careful not to cut your
finger with that **knife**.

小心別被刀子割傷手指。

♤ Do you like potatoes baked or
mashed?

你喜歡烤馬鈴薯還是馬鈴薯
泥?

♤ **Slicing up** onions always brings
tears to my eyes.

切洋蔥時總是令我流眼淚。

＊＊————————————————

leftover 〔'lɛft,ovə〕 *n.* 剩菜;剩飯
mash 〔mæʃ〕 *v.* 搗碎成糊狀

家庭小常識 古人磨刀霍霍向豬羊,聰明的你在切豬肉、牛
肉時可不必磨刀,只要先將菜刀浸在熱水中,
刀刃就鋒利如初,若切魚肉,則先將刀子浸於
鹽水中,切時即可得心應手。

Preparing Meals··

A： I'm busy tonight so *I'll just warm up the leftovers*.
我今晚很忙，所以我只要把剩菜熱一熱。

B： Are you going to play bridge tonight？
妳今晚要去打橋牌嗎？

A： No, that's Tuesday night. Tonight is knitting.
不，星期二晚上才是，今天晚上是織毛衣。

B： You sure keep a full schedule. 妳的時間表總是排得滿滿的！

＊ ＊ ＊

A： *Put a little more garlic powder on that French bread*.
在法國麵包上再灑點大蒜粉。

B： Won't that be a bit too much garlic？
那樣大蒜不會太多嗎？

A： Not at all. The garlic gives it a special *flavor*.
一點也不，大蒜會使麵包有獨特的風味。

＊ ＊ ＊

A： What can I do to help? 我能幫什麼忙嗎？

B： *You can help me toast some bread*.
你可以幫我烤麵包。

A： White bread or wheat bread？ 白麵包還是全麥麵包？

B： About a dozen *slices* of both kinds.
兩種都要，大約烤個十二片。

＊＊─────────────────

knit〔nɪt〕*v*.織毛衣　　schedule〔'skɛdʒʊl〕*n*.時間表

Warm-up

dishrack〔'dɪʃ,ræk〕n. 碗架　　rinse … off 以清水冲洗
dishwasher〔'dɪʃ,wɑʃɚ〕n. 洗碗機
dish towel（ 擦乾碗碟等的 ）抹布

● 洗　碗 ●

♤ Just leave the dishes on the *dishrack* after they've been washed.

碗洗好後，只要放在碗架上就好。

♤ *Rinse* the dishes *off* before you put them in the *dishwasher*.

你要把碗先冲冲水再放進洗碗機。

♤ Let the dishwasher do all the work.

讓洗碗機去洗就好了！

♤ It's really convenient to have a dishwasher.

有一台洗碗機眞的很方便。

♤ It's your turn to *do the dishes*.

該你洗碗了！

♤ These pots and pans are too big to *fit into* the dishwasher.

這些鍋子太大了，洗碗機放不下。

Doing the Dishes··

A : ***Do you have a dishwasher in your house?***
你家有洗碗機嗎？

B : Yes, but the maid doesn't know how to use it.
有，不過女佣不知道怎麼用。

A : Really? 真的？

B : She says there aren't any dishwashers where she is from.
她說她以前在家裏沒有用過洗碗機。

∗   ∗   ∗

A : ***It's your turn to do the dishes.*** 該你洗碗了。

B : No, it's Bobby's turn. 不，該巴比。

A : He has a Cub Scout meeting tonight. His turn is
tomorrow. 他今晚要去開幼童軍大會，明天才輪到他。

B : OK then. As long as he does the dishes tomorrow.
好吧！只要他明天會洗就好了。

**

 Cub Scout 幼童軍 ***as long as*** 只要

家庭小常識 洗米水除了可以擦地板外，用來洗滌泥沙較多的蔬菜，或油膩的碗盤，效果也很好！

Warm-UP

slide in 推進

stove 〔stov〕 *n.* 爐子

microwave 〔'maɪkrə‚wev〕 *n.* 微波

burner 〔'bɜnə〕 *n.* 爐口

oven 〔'ʌvən〕 *n.* 烤箱

gas stove 瓦斯爐

———————● 爐　子 ●———————

♤ Open the oven door and I'll *slide* these *in*.

打開烤箱的門，讓我把這些食物推進去。

♤ Use that *grease remover* to clean the stove.

用去油劑清洗爐子。

♤ The stove needs to be scrubbed.

爐子該刷一刷了！

♤ Don't touch the stove! It's hot.

別碰爐子！很燙哦！

♤ Can you turn off the gas stove?

能不能把瓦斯爐關掉？

＊＊——————————————————

grease 〔gris〕 *n.* 油脂　　　remover 〔rɪ'muvə〕 *n.* 除去物

The Stove, Oven ....

A : ***Open the oven door and I'll slide these in.***
　　打開烤箱的門、讓我把這些推進去。

B : What kind of cookies are they? 這些是什麼餅乾？

A : Peanut butter. 花生奶油的。

B : Oh good. Peanut butter cookies are my favorite.
　　噢，太好了！花生奶油餅乾是我最愛吃的。

　　　　　　　＊　　　　　＊　　　　　＊

A : ***This stove is a gas stove.*** We use it for all our cooking.
　　這一台是瓦斯爐，我們所有的烹調都靠它。

B : You mean you don't have a microwave oven?
　　你是說你們沒有微波爐？

A : Not yet. We're going to buy one next month.
　　還沒有，我們下個月要去買一台。

B : Really? My friend sells them. He can give you a discount.
　　眞的？我的朋友在賣，他可以給你們打折。

**————————————————

discount〔'dɪskaʊnt〕*n.* 折扣

家庭小常識　自製蛋糕西點是餡多味美，但大快朶頤後，面對有油污的烤箱，可別心煩，只要用一隻小碗盛阿摩尼亞水放進去，再將爐門緊閉一夜，次日油垢卽可自動脫除了。

Warm-up

shelf〔ʃɛlf〕*n.* 架

empty〔'ɛmptɪ〕*v.* 使空

get moldy 發霉

fit … in ～ 將…放進～

electricity〔ɪ,lɛk'trɪsətɪ〕*n.* 電

fridge〔frɪdʒ〕*n.* 冰箱（＝refrigerator〔rɪ'frɪdʒə,retə〕）

Saran wrap〔sə'ræn ræp〕*n.* 保鮮膜（＝plastic wrap）

ice cube tray 製冰器

defrost〔di'frɔst〕*v.* 除霜

bottom〔'batəm〕*n.* 底部

cooler〔'kulə〕*n.* 冷藏箱

● 冰 箱 ●

♤ Close the refrigerator door. You're wasting *electricity*.

把冰箱門關上，你在浪費電。

♤ Put all the leftovers in the *fridge*.

把所有剩菜都放到冰箱裏。

♤ Please *empty* the refrigerator.

請清理一下冰箱。

♤ Please get me two eggs from the refrigerator.

請從冰箱拿兩個蛋給我。

♤ The creamer is in the fridge, on the *bottom shelf*.

奶油瓶放在冰箱的最下層。

♤ There's no more ice in the *ice cube tray*.

製冰器裏没有冰塊了。

**

waste〔west〕*v.* 浪費　　creamer〔'krimə〕*n.* 裝奶油的瓶子

♤ You better throw away the cheese. It's beginning to *get moldy*.

你最好把乳酪丟掉，它已經開始發霉了。

♤ Your fruit is rotting in the refrigerator.

你放在冰箱的水果開始爛了。

♤ We need to *defrost* the freezer. The ice is too thick.

冰箱該除霜了，冰太厚了。

♤ I wrapped leftovers with *Saran wrap* and put them away in the refrigerator.

我用保鮮膜把剩菜包起來，再放到冰箱裏去。

♤ This new refrigerator *saves energy*.

這台新冰箱很省電。

♤ That refrigerator is too small. I'll have to *trade* it *in* for a bigger one.

那台冰箱太小了，我要用它去抵購一台更大的。

♤ What's going on in there? Close that refrigerator right now!

裏面到底在幹什麼？立刻關上冰箱！

---

moldy 〔'moldɪ〕*adj.* 發霉的   rot 〔rɑt〕*v.* 腐爛

freezer 〔'frizɚ〕*n.* 冷凍庫   ***trade in*** 抵購

The Refrigerator ··

A : What's for breakfast? 早餐吃什麼？

B : Ham and eggs. ***Please get me two eggs from the refrigerator.*** 火腿蛋，請幫我從冰箱拿出兩個蛋來。

A : OK. Do you need anything else?
好的，還需要別的東西嗎？

B : We're out of orange juice. Can you buy some at the corner store? 柳橙汁沒了，你去街角的店裡買好嗎？

A : Sure. 當然好。

*   *   *

A : ***We need to defrost the freezer. The ice is too thick.***
冰箱該除霜了，冰層太厚了。

B : You're right. I can hardly ***fit*** the ice cream in there any more. 沒錯，我幾乎不能再把冰淇淋放進去了。

A : There's a ***cooler*** with some ice in it over there. Put the ice cream inside the cooler when you defrost the freezer.
那邊有台放冰塊的冷藏箱，在你除霜的時候，就先把冰淇淋放進冷藏箱裡。

B : Good idea! You thought of everything.
好主意，你想得很週到！

家庭小常識　你知道薑湯可以驅寒，但你可能不曉得生薑汁的妙用：肉放在冰箱裏久了會變硬，取出後，可浸在生薑汁中，不但會變得柔軟，而且還能祛腥味。

Warm-up

microwave〔ˈmaɪkrəˌwev〕*n*. 微波（爐）
heat up 加熱

───────● 微波爐 ●───────

♤ Use the **microwave** and it will only take 5 minutes.

用微波爐只要 5 分鐘。

♤ I got a microwave oven for a birthday present.

我生日禮物收到一台微波爐。

♤ It sure is easier to cook with a microwave oven.

用微波爐煮飯的確很簡單。

♤ How long does it take to pop popcorn with a microwave oven?

用微波爐爆玉米花需要多久?

♤ We bought the microwave oven to save time.

為了節省時間我們買了微波爐。

♤ I'll just **heat up** the leftovers in the microwave.

我只要把剩菜放在微波爐裏加熱。

♤ Put some frozen food in the microwave oven.

放一些冷凍食物到微波爐裏。

**──────────────────────

pop〔pɑp〕*v*. 爆炒（玉米等）   save〔sev〕*v*. 節省

The Microwave Oven ·····························

A : It takes 30 minutes to cook this.
　　煮這道菜要花三十分鐘。

B : *Use the microwave and it will only take 5 minutes.*
　　用微波爐只需要五分鐘。

A : A microwave oven sure saves time.
　　用微波爐的確省時間。

　　　　　　　*　　　　　*　　　　　*

A : I've got to be at Aunt Marie's house in an hour.
　　我在一小時內一定要到達瑪琍姑媽家。

B : In that case, *I'll just heat up the leftovers in the micro-
　　wave.* 這樣的話，我就只好用微波爐把剩菜熱一熱了。

A : Good idea. 好主意。

　　　　　　　*　　　　　*　　　　　*

A : I guess, I don't have to waste so much time in cooking,
　　after all. 我想，我終於不需浪費那麼多時間在煮飯上了！

B : How is that so? 怎麼說呢？

A : *I got a microwave oven for a birthday present!*
　　我生日禮物收到一台微波爐。

家庭小常識　潔白光亮的微波爐一旦日久發黃時，可用小蘇
　　　　　　打粉調成薄糊，塗遍爐表的白漆部分，待乾後，
　　　　　　再用軟布抹擦，就能潔白如新。

Warm-up

blender〔'blɛndɚ〕*n.* 攪拌器　　food processor 調理機
toaster〔'tostɚ〕*n.* 烤麵包機　rice cooker 電鍋
can opener 開罐器　　　　　juicer〔'dʒusɚ〕*n.* 榨汁機
mixer〔'mɪksɚ〕*n.* 攪拌機　　coffee maker 咖啡壺

● 食物料理機 ●

♤ Mix all the ingredients in this *blender*.

在攪拌器裏混合所有的原料。

♤ Oh no, the food processor just *broke down*.

糟了，調理機壞了。

♤ Be careful with that *toaster* or you'll burn the toast.

用烤麵包機要注意，否則會把麵包烤焦。

♤ It's easy to use a *rice cooker*.

用電鍋很容易。

♤ Be careful with that *can opener*.

用那個開罐器要小心。

♤ We can use the *juicer* to make orange juice.

我們可以用榨汁機榨一些柳橙汁。

♤ The electric can opener is broken.

這個電動開罐器壞了。

The Food Processor ·······································

A : Mom, where's the can opener? I couldn't find it!
　　媽，開罐器在哪？我怎麼找不到！

B : It's on the dining table. I just left it there. Oh, by the
　　way, ***be careful with that can opener***. It's kind of rusty.
　　在餐桌上，我剛才放的。哦，小心用那個開罐器，因為有點生銹了。

　　　　　　＊　　　　　　　＊　　　　　　　＊

A : I'm so starved. Have you got anything to eat?
　　我好餓，你有沒有東西可以吃？

B : What about some rice? We can cook some rice and I have
　　some canned fish, too.
　　吃飯好嗎？我們可以煮些飯，再配我的魚罐頭。

A : Sounds nice! But are you sure you know how to use a rice
　　cooker?　好像不錯，但你確定你會用電鍋？

B : Why not? ***It's easy to use a rice cooker***.
　　當然！用電鍋很容易。

---

　　rusty〔'rʌstɪ〕*adj.* 生銹的　　　starved〔starvd〕*adj.* 極餓的
　　canned fish 魚罐頭

家庭小常識　用檸檬汁加食鹽來擦拭金屬器皿，不僅可以去銹，並且能擦得光可鑑人。

Warm-up

fresh〔frɛʃ〕*adj.* 新鮮的　　　　have a sale 拍賣

produce〔'prɑdjus〕*n.* 農產品　　shopping center 購物中心

crowded〔'krɑʊdɪd〕*adj.* 擁擠的　section〔'sɛkʃən〕*n.* 區域

clerk〔klɜk〕*n.* 售貨員　　　　daily necessities 日常必需品

sanitary〔'sænə,tɛrɪ〕*adj.* 衛生的 drop in 順便進去

pushcart〔'pʊʃkɑrt〕*n.* 手推車　special offer 特價供應

basement〔'besmənt〕*n.* 地下樓

sanitary articles 衛生用品

air-conditioned〔'ɛrkən'dɪʃənd〕*adj.* 裝有空調設備的

check-out counter （在超市等的）結帳台

coupon〔'kupɑn,'kjupɑn〕*n.* 折價券

──────● 逛超市 ●──────

♤ After the typhoon it's been
hard to find *fresh* vegetables.

颱風過後一直買不到新鮮蔬
菜。

♤ Can you run down to the
supermarket and get me
a loaf of bread?

你能不能跑去超市替我買一
條麵包？

♤ They *have a sale* on coffee
at the supermarket this week.

這家超市本週咖啡特賣。

＊＊────────────

a loaf of 一條

♧ That supermarket is cheaper but their **produce** isn't as fresh.

那家超市比較便宜，但是他們的產品較不新鮮。

♧ The supermarket is located in the **basement** of this **shopping center**.

超市位在這棟購物中心的地下樓。

♧ It's nice to shop in an **air-conditioned** supermarket in the summer.

夏天在有空調的超市裏購物很舒服。

♧ It's better to shop in the supermarket on weekdays, it's not as **crowded**.

平時到超市購物較好，不會那麼擁擠。

♧ Let's drop in the sanitary **section** over there.

我們到那邊的衛生用品區去一下。

**─────────────

locate〔'loket, lo'ket〕*v.* 位於
weekday〔'wik,de〕*n.* 星期日以外的任一天；平日
jasmine〔'dʒæsmɪn,'dʒæz-〕*n.* 茉莉

家庭小常識　從超市買回來的葉菜類蔬菜，別急著放入冰箱。如能先擦乾表面水分，並以報紙包好，再放入冰箱，便能常保生鮮。注意隨時換掉受潮的報紙，以使效果更持久。

Going to the Supermarket ....

A : ***It's nice to shop in an air-conditioned supermarket in the summer*.** 夏天在有空調的超市裏購物眞舒服。

B : That's right. It sure feels nice after being out in the heat. 沒錯。尤其是在炎熱的戶外待過之後，更是覺得舒服。

A : And the vegetables are fresher, too. 蔬菜也比較新鮮。

B : No wonder supermarkets are so popular nowadays. 難怪現在超市這麼受歡迎。

*   *   *

A : Shirley, I'd like to buy some ***daily necessities. Where can I get them***? 雪莉，我想買一些日用品，哪裏可以買得到？

B : What do you want to buy? 你想買什麼？

A : Some sanitary articles. 一些衞生用品。

B : Okay. ***Let's drop in the sanitary section over there.*** 好，我們到那邊的衞生用品區去一下吧！

*   *   *

A : ***They have a sale on coffee at the supermarket this week.*** 這家超市本週咖啡特賣。

B : I've got enough coffee. What about jasmine tea? 我不缺咖啡，那茉莉花茶呢？

A : You'll have to wait until next week when they have a sale on tea. 那得等到下週，那時茶會降價出售。

B : How do you know so much about what's on sale? 你怎麼那麼清楚什麼東西在拍賣？

A : I should know. I work part-time as a clerk there. 我應該知道的，我在那裏打工當店員。

Unit 3

The Garden 花園

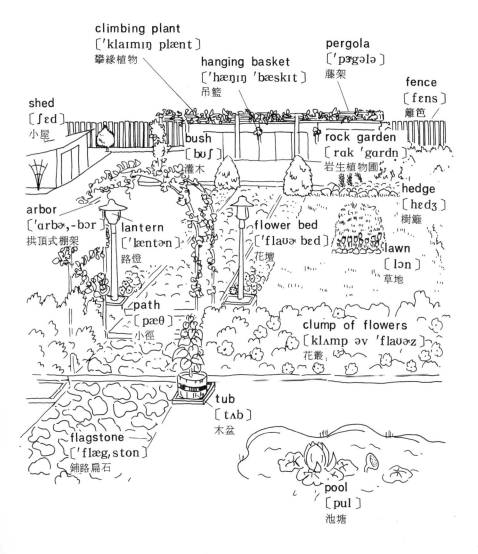

climbing plant
〔'klaımıŋ plænt〕
攀緣植物

hanging basket
〔'hæŋıŋ 'bæskıt〕
吊籃

pergola
〔'pɝgələ〕
藤架

fence
〔fɛns〕
籬笆

shed
〔ʃɛd〕
小屋

bush
〔buʃ〕
灌木

rock garden
〔rɑk 'gɑrdn̩〕
岩生植物圃

hedge
〔hɛdʒ〕
樹籬

arbor
〔'ɑrbɚ,-bɔr〕
拱頂式棚架

lantern
〔'læntən〕
路燈

flower bed
〔'flauɚ bɛd〕
花壇

lawn
〔lɔn〕
草地

path
〔pæθ〕
小徑

clump of flowers
〔klʌmp əv 'flauɚz〕
花叢

tub
〔tʌb〕
木盆

flagstone
〔'flæg,ston〕
鋪路扁石

pool
〔pul〕
池塘

Warm-up

hose〔hoz〕*n*. 橡皮水管　　　lawn-mower 割草機

grass〔græs〕*n*. 草地　　　　seed〔sid〕*n*. 種子

crop〔krɑp〕*n*. 農作物　　　water〔'wɔtɚ,'wɑtɚ〕*v*. 澆水

sow〔so〕*v*. 播種　　　　　sprout〔spraʊt〕*v*. 發芽

mow〔mo〕*v*. 割；刈　　　　lawn〔lɔn〕*n*. 草地

● 園　藝 ●

♠ Our **hose** isn't long enough.　　我們的水管不夠長。

♠ You can **water** the plants.　　你可以替植物澆水。

♠ The **grass** grows so fast.　　草長得太快了。

♠ Please hand me the hose.　　請把水管遞給我。

♠ Are you going to use the **lawn-mower**?　　你要用割草機嗎?

♠ I **sowed** some broad beans two weeks ago.　　我兩個星期前種了一些蠶豆。

♠ The **seeds** are beginning to **sprout**.　　種子開始發芽了。

♠ I hope I can have a good **crop** this year.　　我希望我今年能豐收。

♠ How are your flowers doing?　　你家的花開得如何?

**　　　　　　　　　　

broad bean 蠶豆

Gardening ···

A : **You need to mow the lawn.** 你得去割割草坪的草。

B : Again? The grass grows so fast.
又要割嗎？那些草長得可真快！

A : That's because it's rained a lot lately.
因為最近雨下得太多了。

            *   *   *

A : **The seeds are beginning to sprout.** ·
種子開始發芽了。

B : Already? 已經開始了嗎？

A : Well, the weather's been good this spring.
嗯，今年春天天氣一直不錯。

B : Looks like we'll have fresh garden vegetables to eat this
fall. 看來秋天時我們就會有新鮮的庭園蔬菜可吃了。

A : If the weather is good this summer we sure will.
如果夏天天氣也很好的話，我們一定吃得到。

家庭小常識　不論是自己買的花材，還是人家送的花束，雖然美麗，但往往壽命短暫。若在插花之前，先把花的根部浸在醋中，就可使花莖更易吸水，延長花朵的生命。

Warm-up

barbecue sauce 烤肉醬
grill〔grɪl〕*n.* 烤架
meat〔mit〕*n.* 肉
barbecue〔'barbɪ,kju〕*n. v.* 烤肉
hibachi〔hɪ'batʃɪ〕*n.* 日本之小炭爐

charcoal〔'tʃar,kol〕*n.* 木炭
prawn〔prɔn〕*n.* 明蝦
coat〔kot〕*v.* 塗上

● 烤 肉 ●

♤ I like **barbecued** chicken better than fried chicken.

我比較喜歡烤雞，較不喜歡炸雞。

♤ Make sure you have enough **barbecue sauce**.

你要確定有足夠的烤肉醬。

♤ Does this **charcoal** burn fast?

這木炭燒得很快嗎？

♤ It sure is a nice day for a barbecue.

今天真是烤肉的好日子！

♤ We were going to have a barbecue today but it started raining.

本來我們今天要烤肉，但是卻下起雨來了。

♤ Put more charcoal in the **hibachi**.

在炭爐裏多加點炭。

♤ Bring out the barbecue **grill** from the garage.

把烤肉架從車庫裏搬出來。

♠ Barbecue the prawns for about five minutes.

蝦子烤個五分鐘吧！

♠ The meat was *coated* with too much barbecue sauce.

肉塗太多烤肉醬了。

♠ There's nothing better than barbecued ribs and a cold beer.

沒有什麼比吃烤排骨配冰啤酒更棒的了。

♠ Is there a barbecue pit around here?

這附近有烤肉的坑嗎？

♠ Do you have any barbecue flavor potato chips?

你有烤肉口味的洋芋片嗎？

♠ Please pass me the extra *spicy* barbecue sauce.

請遞給我辣味烤肉醬。

---

ribs〔rɪbz〕*n. pl.* 排骨　　*barbecue pit* 烤全牲用的坑槽
flavor〔'fleva〕*n.* 口味；調味
spicy〔'spaɪsɪ〕*adj.* 辣的

The Barbecue ··

A : *It sure is a nice day for a barbecue.*
今天眞是烤肉的好日子。

B : That's right. I see a lot of other people feel the same
way. 沒錯，其他人也都這麼以爲。

A : It does get a bit crowded here on weekends.
週末時，這裏眞的滿擁擠的。

B : Especially when the weather is good.
天氣好的時候尤其如此。

*　　　　*　　　　*

A : *Did you remember the barbecue sauce?*
你沒忘了帶烤肉醬吧？

B : Oh no, I forgot. I'll get it out of the refrigerator.
啊！眞糟糕，我忘了。我去冰箱裏拿。

A : And bring out the barbecue grill from the garage, too.
同時把烤肉架從車庫裏搬出來。

B : It sure is a lot of work to have a barbecue.
烤肉眞的很費事。

A : But it's worth it. My barbecued chicken is the best in
the county. 但是卻值得呀！我烤的雞肉是本地區最棒的！

Warm-up

tidy〔'taɪdɪ〕adj. 整潔的   rake〔rek〕v. 耙去
paint〔pent〕v. 油漆   fence〔fɛns〕n. 籬笆
make a mess of 弄糟

● 整 理 ●

♤ It sure is difficult to keep the garden *tidy*.

要保持庭院的整潔的確很難。

♤ Who left the gate open?

誰開了門沒關？

♤ It's your turn to *rake* the leaves.

該你去掃樹葉了！

♤ The *fence* needs to be *painted*.

籬笆該油漆了！

♤ Take this bench over to the garden.

把這張長凳搬到院子去。

♤ The dog *made a mess of* the garden. Now we have to tidy it up.

狗把院子弄得一團糟，現在我們得去整理。

Tidying Up ···

A : ***Who left the gate open***？ 誰忘了關大門？

B : Oh, I'm sorry. I forgot. 哦，眞抱歉，是我忘了。

A : We have to be careful. Last year the dog ate some of the flowers. 我們要小心，去年那隻狗就進來吃掉了一些花。

B : Oh dear！ Did the dog get in the garden this time？
我的天！這一次狗又到花園裏來了嗎？

A : No. Good thing the dog is asleep.
那倒沒有，還好那條狗睡著了。

＊ ＊ ＊

A : ***It's your turn to rake the leaves***. 該你耙樹葉了。

B : There sure are a lot of leaves. 一定滿地都是落葉。

A : Most of the leaves fall in October, so next month there won't be many.
大部份的樹葉在十月差不多就掉光了，所以下個月就會比較少。

B : That's good. 眞是太好了。

家庭小常識　容易製造髒亂的煙蒂，其實有不少用途，例如：將之拆開浸水，灑在花木上，可防止病蟲害；將之倒在排水溝旁，則可以避臭除穢。

Unit 4

The Bedroom 臥房

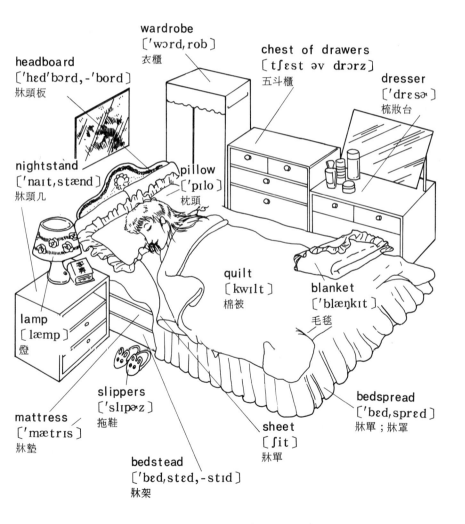

wardrobe
〔'wɔrd,rob〕
衣櫃

chest of drawers
〔tʃɛst əv drɔrz〕
五斗櫃

dresser
〔'drɛsə〕
梳妝台

headboard
〔'hɛd'bɔrd,-'bord〕
牀頭板

nightstand
〔'naɪt,stænd〕
牀頭几

pillow
〔'pɪlo〕
枕頭

lamp
〔læmp〕
燈

quilt
〔kwɪlt〕
棉被

blanket
〔'blæŋkɪt〕
毛毯

mattress
〔'mætrɪs〕
牀墊

slippers
〔'slɪpəz〕
拖鞋

sheet
〔ʃit〕
牀單

bedspread
〔'bɛd,sprɛd〕
牀單；牀罩

bedstead
〔'bɛd,stɛd,-stɪd〕
牀架

Warm-up

pigsty〔'pɪg,staɪ〕 *n.* 豬窩	mattress〔'mætrɪs〕 *n.* 牀墊
sun〔sʌn〕 *v.* 曬太陽	air〔ɛr〕 *v.* 晾乾
fitted sheets 牀罩	drawer〔drɔr〕 *n.* 抽屜
make the bed 整理牀舖	quilt〔kwɪlt〕 *n.* 棉被
pillow〔'pɪlo〕 *n.* 枕頭	tuck〔tʌk〕 *v.* 塞進
cover〔'kʌvɚ〕 *n.* 套子	pull〔pʊl〕 *v.* 拉
smooth〔smuð〕 *v.* 弄平	carpet sweeper 掃毯器
pillowcase〔'pɪlo,kes〕 *n.* 枕頭套	
bedcover〔'bɛd,kʌvɚ〕 *n.* 床單　blanket〔'blæŋkɪt〕 *n.* 毛毯	

───●　打　掃　●───

♤ Clean up this room. It looks like a *pigsty*.	打掃一下房間！看起來像個豬窩。
♤ The *mattress* needs to be *sunned* and *aired* outside.	牀墊應該搬出去曬曬太陽，通通風。
♤ The *fitted sheets* are in that *drawer*.	牀罩在那個抽屜裏。
♤ Will you help me *make the bed*?	你可以幫我舖牀嗎？
♤ I don't think we need this heavy *quilt* anymore.	我認為我們不需要再蓋厚棉被了。
♤ Should I change the sheets and *pillowcases*?	我該換牀單和枕頭套了嗎？

♤ ***Tuck in*** the sheet.　　　　　　把牀單塞進去。

♤ It's time to change the　　　　　該換枕頭套了！
pillow ***covers***.

♤ ***Pull*** out that corner a bit.　　從那一角拉出來一點。

♤ ***Smooth out*** the wrinkles　　把牀單上的皺褶攤平。
from that sheet.

♤ The ***bedcover*** needs to be　　牀單該洗了！
washed.

♤ Do we have any clean sheets?　　我們有乾淨的牀單嗎？

♤ I'll need another ***blanket*** soon.　我得趕快添件毯子，冬天就
It's almost winter.　　　　　　　要來了。

♤ Make sure the baby has enough　寶寶睡覺時，一定要給他蓋
blankets covering him when he's　上足夠的毯子。
asleep.

♤ Oh no! The cat shed all over　　糟糕！毯子上都是猫咪脫落
the blanket!　　　　　　　　　的毛！

**—————————

wrinkle 〔'rɪŋkl〕 *n.* 皺褶　　shed 〔ʃɛd〕 *v.* 脫毛

Cleaning Up ···

A : **Clean up this room! It looks like a pigsty!**
　　打掃一下房間！看起來眞像個豬窩！

B : That's because I'm a big pig. 那是因爲我是頭大豬。

A : No, you're a little pig. Your father is a big pig.
　　不，你是頭小豬，你爸爸才是大豬。

B : Oink, oink. （豬叫聲。）

A : Like father, like son. 眞是有其父必有其子。

　　　　　　＊　　　　　　＊　　　　　　＊

A : **Will you help me make the bed?** 你可以幫我舖床嗎？

B : Sure. You mean you don't know how to make a bed?
　　當然可以。你是說你不知道如何舖床嗎？

A : No, I don't. We had a maid when I was growing up.
　　的確，我不知道。從小到大，一直有僕人服侍我。

B : It's easy. Here, I'll show you how.
　　很簡單的。來，我教你怎麼舖。

＊＊————————————

　maid〔med〕n. 女僕

家庭小常識　一不小心打翻墨水瓶，弄髒地毯時，別著慌，可將食鹽灑在墨水漬上，等濕了後清掉，再灑上乾的食鹽，直到墨水被吸淨後，再用肥皂水清洗卽可。

Warm-up

rise〔raɪz〕v. 起（床）　　　go to bed 就寢
keep late hours 晚睡晚起　　toss〔tɔs〕v. 輾轉反側
nightmare〔'naɪt,mɛr〕n. 惡夢　stretch〔strɛtʃ〕v. 伸懶腰
oversleep〔'ovə,slip〕v. 睡眠過久
alarm（clock）〔ə'lɑrm〕n. 鬧鐘
soundly〔'saʊndlɪ〕adv. 熟地；安穩地

● 休息・起牀 ●

♤ Early to bed and early to **rise** makes a man healthy, wealthy and wise.

早睡早起使人健康、富裕而聰明。

♤ Make it a rule to **go to bed** at 9.

要養成九點睡覺的習慣。

♤ Don't **keep late hours**.

別晚睡晚起。

♤ You have to get up early for school.

你必須早起上學。

♤ I feel sleepy.

我想睡覺。

♤ Don't smoke in bed.

別在牀上抽煙。

＊＊

wealthy〔'wɛlθɪ〕adj. 富裕的　　wise〔waɪz〕adj. 聰明的

♤ It's important to get enough rest when you have a cold.　感冒時有充份的休息很重要。

♤ I *overslept* because I forgot to set the *alarm*.　我睡過頭是因爲忘了設定鬧鐘。

♤ I was *tossing* and turning all night.　我整晚輾轉反側。

♤ I had trouble falling asleep.　我睡不著。

♤ I had horrible *nightmares*.　我做了惡夢。

♤ I slept *soundly*.　我睡得很熟。

♤ I always *stretch* after I get out of bed.　我起牀後總會伸伸懶腰。

**──────────

horrible〔ˈhɔrəbḷ, ˈhɑrəbḷ〕*adj.* 可怕的

大字型
sleep stretched

蜷縮身子
sleep curled up

側睡
sleep on one's side

仰睡
sleep on one's back

俯睡
sleep on one's stomach

Resting, Waking Up ·······························

A : **I can't seem to get up early in the morning.**
　　早晨我似乎總是無法早起。

B : When do you usually go to sleep? 你通常何時就寢？

A : Sometime after the late night show on TV.
　　看完電視上的午夜節目後才睡。

B : You should make it a rule to go to bed by 11.
　　你應該養成十一點前上床的習慣。

　　　　　　＊　　　　　＊　　　　　＊

A : Well, what is it, Doc? 嗯，醫生，是什麼病？

B : Nothing serious, you just have a common cold.
　　不嚴重，你只是患了普通的感冒。

A : Do I have to take any pills? 我得吃藥嗎？

B : No, not at all. Drink plenty of water and eat **nutritious**
　　food. 不，不用。多喝開水，多吃些營養的食物。

A : What else? 還有呢？

B : **It's important to get enough rest when you have a cold.**
　　感冒時，充份休息也是很重要的。

Doc〔dɑk〕*n.* (俚) 醫生 (＝Doctor)　　pill〔pɪl〕*n.* 藥丸
nutritious〔nju'trɪʃəs〕*adj.* 滋養的

Warm-up

electric fan 電扇	air conditioner 冷氣機
floor fan 落地扇	desk fan 桌扇
space heater 小暖爐	turn on 打開
rotate〔'rotet〕v. 旋轉	heat〔hit〕n. 暖氣
electricity〔ɪ,lɛk'trɪsətɪ〕n. 電	

●── 冷氣機・暖氣機・電風扇 ●─────

♤ There is nothing like an **electric fan** in summer.

夏天時，沒有比電扇更重要的了。

♤ An **air conditioner** is essential in the summertime.

在夏天，冷氣機是不可或缺的。

♤ Will you let the **floor fan rotate**?

你讓落地扇旋轉好嗎？

♤ Turn on the **desk fan**.

把桌扇打開。

♤ That **space heater** uses up a lot of electricity.

那個小暖爐很耗電。

✽✽────────────

essential〔ə'sɛnʃəl〕adj. 必要的
summertime〔'sʌmɚ,taɪm〕n. 夏季

Air Conditioner, Heater, Fan ·······················

A : It sure is hot today. 今天真熱。

B : It's a good thing this apartment has an air conditioner.
這間公寓有冷氣真好。

A : That's right. ***An air conditioner is essential in the summer.***
沒錯，夏天真是少不了冷氣。

*　　　　*　　　　*

A : Turn the ***heat*** up, will you？ I'm freezing !
把暖氣開強一點好嗎？我好冷！

B : But did you see our last heating bill ?
可是你看到我們上個月吹暖氣的電費了嗎？

A : So what should I do, freeze to death ?
那我該怎麼辦？凍死嗎？

B : No, put on a sweater. 不，穿件毛衣吧。

---

freezing〔'frizɪŋ〕*adj.* 寒冷的；冷凍的
heating〔'hitɪŋ〕*n.* 暖氣　　bill〔bɪl〕*n.* 帳單

Unit 5

The Garage 車庫

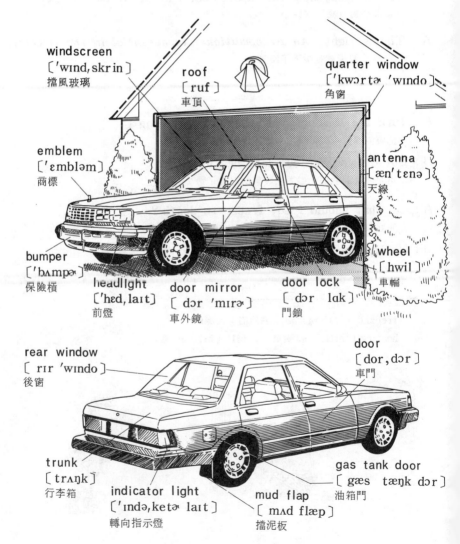

windscreen
〔'wɪnd,skrin〕
擋風玻璃

roof
〔ruf〕
車頂

quarter window
〔'kwɔrtɚ 'wɪndo〕
角窗

emblem
〔'ɛmbləm〕
商標

antenna
〔æn'tɛnə〕
天線

bumper
〔'bʌmpɚ〕
保險槓

headlight
〔'hɛd,laɪt〕
前燈

door mirror
〔dɔr 'mɪrɚ〕
車外鏡

door lock
〔dɔr lɑk〕
門鎖

wheel
〔hwil〕
車輪

rear window
〔rɪr 'wɪndo〕
後窗

door
〔dor,dɔr〕
車門

trunk
〔trʌŋk〕
行李箱

indicator light
〔'ɪndə,ketɚ laɪt〕
轉向指示燈

mud flap
〔mʌd flæp〕
擋泥板

gas tank door
〔gæs tæŋk dɔr〕
油箱門

Warm-up

tune-up〔'tjun,ʌp〕*n*. 調整　　repair〔rɪ'pɛr〕*v*. 修理
align〔ə'laɪn〕*v*. 排成直錢　wheel〔hwil〕*n*. 輪子
snow tire 雪上輪胎　　　　wrench〔rɛntʃ〕*n*. 螺絲扳手
screw〔skru〕*n*. 螺絲　　engine〔'ɛndʒən〕*n*. 引擎
screw driver 螺絲起子　　brake〔brek〕*n*. 煞車
bumper〔'bʌmpɚ〕*n*. 保險桿　emergency brake 緊急煞車
headlamp〔'hɛd,læmp〕*n*. 車頭燈（＝headlight）
taillight〔'tel,laɪt〕*n*. 尾燈（＝rear light）

————● 汽車修護 ●————

♤ This car needs a ***tune-up***.

這部車需要調整。

♤ It's a fast car but it has to be ***repaired*** often.

這部車跑得很快，但卻需要經常送修。

♤ Can you ***align*** the ***wheels***?

你能不能幫我把車輪調正？

♤ It's almost winter, I'd better change to ***snow tires***.

冬天快到了，我看最好是換上雪上輪胎。

♤ We don't have a ***wrench*** that size. We'll have to buy one.

我們沒有那種尺寸的扳手，必須去買一個。

♤ Make sure your ***emergency brake*** is on before you start the car.

你要確定緊急利車系統沒問題，才可以上路。

♤ My front right ***headlamp*** is broken. Have you got an extra one?

我車子右前方的車燈壞了，你有沒有備用的？

Car Maintenance ························

A : So how do you like your Ferrari?
  你覺得你那輛法拉利如何呢？

B : *It's a fast car but parts are expensive.*
  車子是跑得很快，不過零件太貴了。

A : So why do you spend so much money on the car?
  那麼你為什麼要花這麼多錢在這部車子上？

B : You should see the looks I get from women when I'm
  driving it. 你真該看看我開這部車子時，那些女人們看我的表情。

A : Oh, I see. 哦，我懂了。

*   *   *

A : Hey, can you listen to this funny noise coming from my
  engine? 嗨，你來聽聽看我車子引擎所發出來的怪聲好嗎？

B : *This car needs a tune-up.* 這部車需要調整一番。

A : Will it take long? 要很久嗎？

B : No, just about twenty minutes. 不用，二十分鐘就好了。

家庭小常識　汽車內各角落的灰塵髒物要清除不容易，可利用舊的衣服刷子，會比掃帚來得有效。要是汽車坐墊染上髒污，則用含有甘油脂的清潔劑擦拭即可。

Warm-up

stock up on 購存
canned〔kænd〕*adj.* 罐裝的
spare〔spɛr〕*adj.* 備用的

store〔stor, stɔr〕*v.* 貯藏
toolbox〔'tul,baks〕*n.* 工具箱
parts〔parts〕*n. pl.* 零件

● 儲藏物品 ●

♤ We better ***stock up on*** frozen food for the holidays.

我們最好購存冷凍食品，以便假日時食用。

♤ I always ***store*** some ***canned*** food for emergencies.

我總是貯存一些罐頭食品以備不時之需。

♤ I can never find things when I need them.

我需要的東西老是找不到。

♤ The broom is in that closet.

掃把在櫥櫃裏。

♤ I keep all my tools in that ***toolbox***.

我把所有的工具放在工具箱中。

♤ I keep some ***spare parts*** in this box.

我將些備用的零件放入這箱子內。

＊＊

emergency〔ɪ'mɝdʒənsɪ〕*n.* 緊急需要
broom〔brum〕*n.* 掃帚

Storing Things ·······································

A : Did you hear that another typhoon is coming？
　　你有沒有聽到又有個颱風要來了？

B : Yes, I heard it on the radio a few minutes ago.
　　有，幾分鐘前我聽收音機報導過了。

A : I bought some candles and batteries just in case.
　　我買了些蠟燭、電池以防萬一。

B : *I always store some canned food for emergencies.*
　　我總是購存一些罐頭食品以備不時之需。

　　　　　　＊　　　　　　＊　　　　　　＊

A : My front right headlamp is broken. Have you got an extra
　　one？ 我車子右前方的車燈壞了，你有沒有一個備用的？

B : I don't know, I'll check. 不太清楚，我找找看。

A : Where do you keep your spare parts？
　　你的備用零件都放在哪兒？

B : *I keep some spare parts in this box.*
　　我放了一些在這箱子裏。

**

candle〔'kænd!〕*n.* 蠟燭　　*in case* 以防萬一

家庭小常識　鋸子使用過後，時日一久難免會生銹，鋸起來就不靈光。這裡有一招鋸子防銹術：使用過後，把沾在表面的木屑等清除乾淨，然後再以脫脂棉沾上沙拉油擦拭即可。

Warm-up

──────── ● 個人工作室 ● ────────

♤ This **workbench** is really **handy**.

這工作檯眞的很方便。

♤ Do you do all your **repairs** in this shop?

你都在這個工作室裏修理東西嗎？

♤ This is his workroom. He's a real jack of all trades.

這裏是他的工作室，他眞是個萬事通。

♤ Have you seen my adjustable **wrench**?

你有沒有看過我的可調式螺絲扳手？

♤ The wrenches are all in my **toolbox**.

螺絲扳手都在我的工具箱裏。

♤ We'll have to go to the hardware store. I'm all out of nails.

我們得去趟五金行，我的釘子用完了。

＊＊────────────────

jack of all trades 萬事通；博而不精的人
adjustable〔əˈdʒʌstəb!〕*adj.* 可調整的　**hardware store** 五金行

The Personal Workshop ·····························

A： ***Do you do all your repairs in this shop***？
　　你都在這個工作室裏修理東西嗎？

B： That's right. I've done it this way for years.
　　沒錯，幾年來都是如此。

A： Have you ever thought of moving into a bigger shop？
　　有沒有想過搬到大一點的工作室呢？

B： Not at all. I like it here, it's kind of quaint.
　　沒想過，蠻奇怪的，我就是喜歡在這裏做。

　　　　　　＊　　　　　　　＊　　　　　　　＊

A： My watch stopped. Can you fix it？　我的錶停了，你能幫我修嗎？

B： No problem.　沒問題。

A： Can you fix it here？　I need it fixed by tomorrow.
　　可不可以在這兒修？明天以前一定要修好。

B： Actually ***I do most of the repairs here myself***.
　　事實上我幾乎都自己在這裏修東西。

A： What about this watch？　這錶有什麼問題嗎？

B： Let's see...nothing complicated. You'll have it by to-
　　morrow.　我看看…不會很複雜，明天以前就可以修好。

＊＊———————————————

　　quaint〔kwent〕*adj.* 古怪有趣的
　　complicated〔'kɑmpləˌketɪd〕*adj.* 複雜的

家庭小常識　釘釘子看似簡單，但要做起來省力輕鬆，可是
有秘訣的哦！釘釘子時，先把釘子插在肥皂裏，
拔出後再釘，可就省力多了。

Unit 6

The Dining Room 飯廳

sideboard
〔'saɪd,bord〕
餐具架

dining chair
〔'daɪnɪŋ tʃɛr〕
餐椅

candle
〔'kændl̩〕
蠟燭

plate
〔plet〕
盤子

chopsticks
〔'tʃɑp,stɪks〕
筷子

fork
〔fɔrk〕
叉

spoon
〔spun〕
湯匙

knife
〔naɪf〕
刀

napkin
〔'næpkɪn〕
餐巾

vacuum bottle
〔'vækjʊəm 'bɑtl̩〕
熱水瓶

butter container
〔'bʌtɚ kən'tenɚ〕
奶油罐

glass
〔glæs〕
玻璃杯

caster
〔'kæstɚ〕
調味瓶

tablecloth
〔'tebl̩,klɔθ〕
桌巾

coffee cup
〔'kɔfɪ kʌp〕
咖啡杯

bread basket
〔brɛd 'bæskɪt〕
麵包籃

coffee pot
〔'kɔfɪ pɑt〕
咖啡壺

Warm-up

spoon〔spun〕*n.* 湯匙
fork〔fɔrk〕*n.* 叉子
soup〔sup〕*n.* 湯
set〔sɛt〕*v.* 準備
chopsticks〔'tʃɑp͵stɪks〕*n. pl.* 筷子
tablecloth〔'tebl͵klɔθ〕*n.* 桌巾

bowl〔bol〕*n.* 碗
drinking glass 玻璃杯
napkin〔'næpkɪn〕*n.* 餐巾
run out of 缺（貨）

● 準備用餐 ●

♤ Please put the **soup** on the table.

請把湯擺在飯桌上。

♤ We've **run out of spoons** and **chopsticks**.

湯匙和筷子不夠用了。

♤ The **drinking glass** goes to the right.

喝飲料用的玻璃杯請放到右邊。

♤ Do you know how to fold **napkins**?

你知道如何摺餐巾嗎？

♤ Bring us another **fork**.

請拿給我們另一副叉子。

♤ The table is all **set**.

飯桌都擺設好了。

♤ We only use the **tablecloth** on special occasions.

只有在特別的場合裡，我們才用桌巾。

♤ We've run out of paper napkins.

餐巾紙用完了。

Setting the Table ··

A： Oh no. **We've run out of spoons**. 噢！糟糕！湯匙不夠用了。

B： Don't worry. There are more in that drawer.
別擔心，那抽屜裏還有。

A： We sure have a lot of guests tonight.
今晚來的客人一定很多。

B： We do every Thanksgiving. 每年的感恩節都是如此。

    *   *   *

A： Where do I put this glass？ 這杯子我該放哪兒？

B： **The drinking glass goes to the right**.
喝飲料用的杯子放在右邊。

A： How many spoons are there？ 該有幾根湯匙？

B： Two. One is a soup spoon and the other a dessert spoon.
兩根。一根是喝湯用的，而另一根是用來吃甜點。

**——————————————

fold〔fold〕*v.* 摺疊　　occasion〔ə'keʒən〕*n.* 場合
drawer〔drɔr〕*n.* 抽屜　　Thanksgiving〔,θæŋks'gɪvɪŋ〕*n.* 感恩節
dessert〔dɪ'zɝt〕*n.* 餐後的甜點

家庭小常識　你常為粗心打破碗盤、玻璃器皿而煩惱嗎？

——只要把新買回來的碗盤和玻璃杯等，
先置於鹽水中煮過，就不易破裂了！——

Warm-up

serve〔sɜv〕*v*. 擺（食物）　　main course 主菜
meal〔mil〕*n*. 餐　　　　　　slice〔slaɪs〕*n*. 片
appetizer〔'æpə,taɪzə〕*n*. 開胃菜
dessert〔dɪ'zɜt〕*n*. 餐後的甜點
brunch〔brʌntʃ〕*n*. 早午餐（breakfast＋lunch）
bon appétit〔bɔ̃ ɑpe'ti〕（法）（祝你）胃口大開

─────● 上　菜 ●─────

♧ Here's some juice to quench your thirst.

這是一些讓你解渴的果汁。

♧ **Serve** the **appetizers** first, then the **main course**.

先上開胃菜,然後再上主菜。

♤ It's sure convenient to have a maid serve **meals**.

有僕人做菜的確很方便。

♤ Steak will be served for the main course.

牛排是主菜。

♤ Meals are served at 7 o'clock sharp.

七點正上菜。

───────────────────

quench** one's **thirst 解渴　　maid〔med〕*n*. 女僕
steak〔stek〕*n*. 牛排　　sharp〔ʃɑrp〕*adv*. 準;整

♤ Bring me a glass of water, please.　　　　請給我一杯水 。

♤ That's a big *slice* you're giving me.　　　你給我好大一片 ！

♤ *Dessert* will be served after the main course.　　　主菜上完後再上甜點 。

♤ I'll serve lunch.　　　　午餐我負責供應 。

♤ If you haven't had breakfast, join us for *brunch*.　　如果你還沒吃早餐，跟我們一起去吃早午餐吧 ！

♤ Dinner is ready.　　　　晚餐已備妥 。

♤ Come down and eat your breakfast.　　　下來吃早餐 。

Serving Meals ···

A : Clive, what will we have for dinner this evening?
克利夫，我們今天晚上吃什麼？

B : ***Steak will be served for the main course***, sir.
牛排是主菜，先生。

A : And what about dessert? 那甜點呢？

B : Dessert will be fresh strawberries and cream.
甜點是新鮮的草莓和鮮奶油。

A : Very good, Clive. 很好，克利夫。

B : Bon appétit, sir. 祝您胃口大開，先生。

*　　　*　　　*

A : ***It's sure convenient to have a maid serve meals.***
有僕人做菜眞方便。

B : I know. Me and my husband both work so it's a big help.
我知道。我和我先生都在上班，所以有僕人幫助很大。

————————————

strawberry〔'strɔ,bɛrɪ,-bərɪ〕*n.* 草莓　　cream〔krim〕*n.* 鮮奶油

家庭小常識　荷包蛋要煎得完整不容易，但只要略施小技，在煎荷包蛋時，先在炸熱的油上灑些麵粉，這樣就可防止荷包蛋破裂了。

Warm-up

taste〔test〕*n.* 口味
plain〔plen〕*adj.*（食物）平淡的
sweet〔swit〕*adj.* 甜的
hot〔hɑt〕*adj.* 辣的
pepper〔'pɛpɚ〕*n.* 胡椒粉
salt〔sɔlt〕*n.* 鹽
toothpick holder 牙籤罐
holder〔'holdɚ〕*n.* 容器
add〔æd〕*v.* 添加
have room for 吃得下
greasy〔'grisɪ,'grizɪ〕*adj.* 油膩的
heavy〔'hɛvɪ〕*adj.*（味道）重的；強烈的
spaghetti〔spə'gɛtɪ〕*n.* 義大利麵條
lasagna〔lə'zɑnjə〕*n.* 義大利千層寬麵
highchair〔'haɪ,tʃɛr〕*n.* 供幼童使用的高腳椅
fabulous〔'fæbjələs〕*adj.* 神奇的
stringy〔'strɪŋɪ〕*adj.*（肉等）多筋的

spicy〔'spaɪsɪ〕*adj.* 芳香的
bland〔blænd〕*adj.* 無味的
salty〔'sɔltɪ〕*adj.* 鹹的
full〔fʊl〕*adj.* 飽的
gravy〔'grevɪ〕*n.* 肉汁
knife〔naɪf〕*n.* 刀子
toothpick〔'tuθ,pɪk〕*n.* 牙籤
pass〔pæs,pɑs〕*v.* 傳遞
slurp〔slɝp〕*v.* 啜食時發出響聲
hit the spot 合口味；使人滿意

● 吃 ●

♤ I'm hungry / full. | 我餓了／吃飽了。

♤ Do you need a **highchair** for the baby? | 需要給小孩坐的高腳椅嗎？

♤ Could you **pass** the **salt**? | 請把鹽遞給我，好嗎？

♤ Never point a **knife** at someone. | 不准拿刀子指著別人。

♤ Don't talk with your mouth **full**. | 滿口都是食物時不要開口說話。

♤ The **toothpick holder** is on the counter.

裝牙籤的容器在櫃枱上。

♤ Eating grilled hamburger is much healthier.

吃烤過的漢堡比較健康。

♤ Oh, it **tastes spicy** (greasy／heavy／plain／sweet／salty／hot).

噢,吃起來香辣夠味(真油／口味真重／味道真淡／真甜／真鹹／真辣)。

♤ I must taste that pie. It looks delicious.

那塊派看起來很好吃的樣子,我一定要嚐一嚐。

♤ What a **fabulous** cook you are!

你真是位神奇的廚師!

♤ You're very good at making **spaghetti**.

你的義大利麵做得很好吃。

♤ You can **add** salt and **pepper** to suit your taste.

你可依自己的口味,加鹽和胡椒粉。

♤ Can I have some more **gravy**?

我可以再要一些肉汁嗎?

♤ This dessert is delicious.

這甜點真好吃。

♤ I can't eat anymore.

我吃不下了。

---

counter〔'kaʊntɚ〕 n. 櫃枱　　grill〔grɪl〕 v. 炙;烤
pie〔paɪ〕 n. 派

♠ This meat is **stringy**!

這肉吃起來很多筋。

♠ Don't make **slurping** noises when you eat soup.

喝湯時別發出怪聲。

♠ I always **have room for** dessert.

我總是吃得下甜點。

♠ Ah! That hits the spot.

啊,那正好合我的口味。

♠ I'm so hungry that I could eat a whole chicken!

我餓死了!(我餓得可以吃下一整隻雞。)

♠ Here's some popcorn to munch on before the food arrives.

飯菜送上來之前,先吃這些爆米花。

♠ Stop playing with your food!

不要邊吃邊玩!

＊＊

popcorn 〔'pɑp,kɔrn〕 *n.* 爆米花   munch 〔mʌntʃ〕 *v.* 大聲咀嚼

Eating ....

A：***You're very good at making spaghetti***. It's delicious.
　　你很會做義大利麵，真好吃！

B：Thanks. Actually it's easy to make spaghetti.
　　謝謝！事實上義大利麵很容易做。

A：Can you make lasagna? 你會做義大利千層寬麵嗎？

B：Now that's a little bit more difficult.
　　這道菜就比較難一點了。

　　　　　　　　＊　　　　　　＊　　　　　　＊

A：How is the soup? 湯的味道如何呢？

B：It's a little bland. 味道有點淡。

A：***You can add salt and pepper to suit your taste***.
　　你可以依自己的口味，加鹽和胡椒。

　　　　　　　　＊　　　　　　＊　　　　　　＊

A：***I'm so hungry that I could eat a whole chicken***! How
　　much longer would you take to finish cooking？
　　我餓死了！你還要多久才能煮好？

B：At least another hour. But, here's some popcorn to munch
　　on before the food arrives.
　　至少還要一小時。不過，飯菜送上來前，先吃些爆米花吧！

A：Gee！ Thanks！ 哇！謝了！

家庭小常識　飯後一杯茶可幫助消化、養顏美容、防止蛀牙，但如果你的腸胃不好，切忌飲下過量的茶，否則會造成負面的刺激，反而成為胃腸的額外負擔。

Warm-up

take away 拿走   put away 收拾整齊
wipe〔waɪp〕*v.* 擦

──────●清理餐桌●──────

♤ Can you ***take away*** the dishes?   把菜收走好嗎?

♤ Please put it away.   請收拾好。

♤ Clear the table.   清理餐桌。

♤ This tablecloth needs to be   桌布該換了。
   changed.

♤ I'm tired of washing the dishes.   我很討厭洗碗。

♤ Are these dishes real china?   這些碗盤是真的瓷器嗎?

♤ Where do I put these wine   這些酒杯要放在哪兒?
   glasses?

♤ That was really a good meal.   這一餐吃得真豐盛。

＊＊ ──────────────

be tired of 厭倦   china〔'tʃaɪnə〕*n.* 瓷器

Clearing the Table ·······

A : ***Can you take away the dishes***? I'll wipe the table.
你把菜收走好嗎？我要擦桌子。

B : No problem. Who will wash the dishes?
沒問題。那誰洗碗呢？

A : It's Joey's turn today.
今天該喬伊了。

*   *   *

A : ***I'm tired of washing the dishes***. 我很討厭洗碗。

B : Somebody's got to do it. 總得有人洗啊！

A : But why me? 但為什麼我洗？

B : Because you can't cook, that's why.
就是因為你不會作菜。

*   *   *

A : ***That was really a good meal***. 這一餐吃得眞豐盛。

B : Too bad now we have to wash the pots and pans.
糟糕的是現在我們還得洗這些碗盤。

A : What we need is a maid. 我們需要一個佣人。

B : On my salary? Forget it!
就拿我這點薪水？算了吧！

Warm-up

surprise〔sə'praɪz〕 n. 驚喜   toast〔tost〕 v.,n. 乾杯
cheer〔tʃɪr〕 v. 喝采；歡呼   bottoms up 乾杯
congratulation〔kən͵grætʃə'leʃən〕 n. 祝賀
bravo〔'brɑvo〕 int. 要得；好極了
anniversary〔͵ænə'vɜsərɪ〕 n. 週年紀念

● 慶 祝 ●

♤ *Surprise*! Happy birthday!   大驚喜！生日快樂！

♤ It's too bad Christmas only comes once a year.   眞是太可惜了，聖誕節一年才只有一次。

♤ *Congratulations* on your pro-motion! Let's have a *toast*.   恭喜你升遷了！乾杯！

♤ We all *cheered* our baseball team.   我們全部都爲我國棒球代表隊加油。

♤ We cheered the news that he was elected governor.   他當選首長的消息令我們歡欣鼓舞。

♤ *Bravo*!   好極了！

** promotion〔prə'moʃən〕 n. 升遷   governor〔'gʌvənə〕 n. 首長

♤ Let's toast our anniversary! 　　爲我們的紀念日乾杯 。

♤ I got this as a gift of con-　　這是別人祝賀我的禮物 。
gratulations.

♤ I finally got my promotion.　　我終於升遷了 , 咱們來慶祝
Let's celebrate.　　　　　　　吧 !

♤ The fans really went wild after　　在該隊贏得冠軍後 , 支持他
their team won the champion-　　們的球迷們眞的瘋狂了 。
ship.

♤ "Five , four , three , two , one…　　五秒、四秒、三秒、二秒、
Happy new year ! "　　　　　　一秒…新年快樂 !

＊＊────────────

celebrate〔'sɛlə,bret〕*v.* 慶祝　　***go wild*** 發狂
championship〔'tʃæmpɪən,ʃɪp〕*n.* 冠軍

Celebrations ···

A : ***Congratulations on your promotion! Let's have a toast.***
　　恭喜你升遷了！乾杯！

B : I was really surprised when the boss told me.
　　老板告訴我時，我眞的很驚訝。

A : Well, bottoms up! 嗯，乾杯吧！

　　　　　　＊　　　　　＊　　　　　＊

A : ***Surprise! Happy birthday!***
　　大驚喜！生日快樂！

B : And I thought you guys forgot.
　　我還以爲你們忘了呢。

A : How could we forget? 怎麼可能忘？

***

boss〔bɔs〕*n.* 老板　　guy〔gaɪ〕*n.* 人；傢伙

Unit 7

The Bathroom 浴室

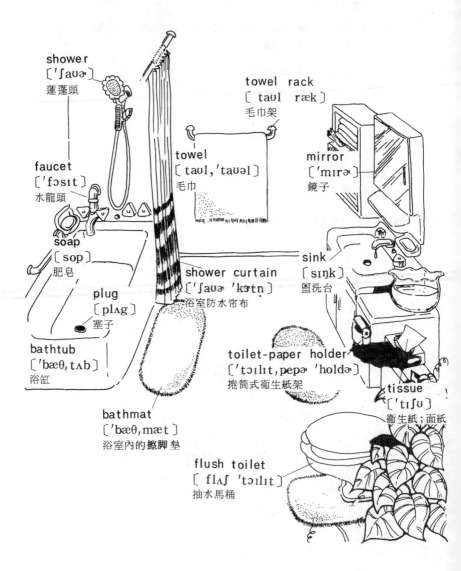

shower
〔'ʃaʊɚ〕
蓮蓬頭

towel rack
〔taʊl ræk〕
毛巾架

faucet
〔'fɔsɪt〕
水龍頭

towel
〔taʊl, 'taʊəl〕
毛巾

mirror
〔'mɪrɚ〕
鏡子

soap
〔sop〕
肥皂

sink
〔sɪŋk〕
盥洗台

shower curtain
〔'ʃaʊɚ 'kɝtn〕
浴室防水帘布

plug
〔plʌg〕
塞子

bathtub
〔'bæθ,tʌb〕
浴缸

toilet-paper holder
〔'tɔɪlɪt,pepɚ 'holdɚ〕
捲筒式衛生紙架

tissue
〔'tɪʃu〕
衛生紙；面紙

bathmat
〔'bæθ,mæt〕
浴室內的擦脚墊

flush toilet
〔flʌʃ 'tɔɪlɪt〕
抽水馬桶

Warm-up

take a bath 洗澡（盆浴）

water heater 熱水器

flush〔flʌʃ〕*v.* 沖洗

flush toilet 抽水馬桶

bath towel 浴巾

soap〔sop〕*n.* 肥皂

sink〔sɪŋk〕*n.* 洗臉台

hair dryer 吹風機

drain〔dren〕*n.* 水管

bath tub 浴盆；浴缸（＝bathtub）

shampoo〔ʃæmˈpu〕*v.* 洗頭　　*n.* 洗髮精

shower〔ˈʃauɚ〕*n.* 淋浴用之蓮蓬頭

toothbrush〔ˈtuθ,brʌʃ〕*n.* 牙刷

toothpaste〔ˈtuθ,pest〕*n.* 牙膏

conditioner〔kənˈdɪʃənɚ〕*n.* 整髮劑

toilet paper 衛生紙（通常指捲筒狀的）

medicine cabinet 醫藥櫃（通常置洗手台上方）

gargle〔ˈgɑrgl̩〕*v.* 漱口

lazybones〔ˈlezɪ,bonz〕*n.* 懶人；懶骨頭

tepid〔ˈtɛpɪd〕*adj.* 微溫的

pressure〔ˈprɛʃɚ〕*n.* 壓力

toilet〔ˈtɔɪlɪt〕*n.* 廁所

rinse〔rɪns〕*v.* 沖水

towel rack 毛巾架

soap dish 肥皂盒

razor〔ˈrezɚ〕*n.* 剃刀

shave〔ʃev〕*v.* 刮鬍子

soak〔sok〕*v.* 浸；泡

peak〔pik〕*n.* 尖鋒

————● 梳　洗 ●————

♤ *Shampoo* your hair.　　　　洗一洗頭髮。

♤ The *shower* isn't working.　　蓮蓬頭壞了。

♤ I'll *take a bath*.　　　　　我要洗個澡。

♤ The water is still *tepid*.　　水還是溫溫的。

♤ ***Turn on*** the hot water, please.　請打開熱水。

♤ The ***water heater*** isn't working properly.　熱水器故障了。

♤ The water ***pressure*** is a bit low.　水壓低了一點。

♤ Remember to ***flush*** the ***toilet*** after each use.　記得每次上完廁所都得沖水。

♤ ***Rinse*** yourself off before you take a bath.　你洗澡前要先沖沖水。

♤ Where's my ***toothbrush***?　我的牙刷在哪裡？

♤ You need to ***shave***.　你得刮鬍子。

♤ Please ***drain*** the water from the ***sink***.　請把洗臉台的水放掉。

♤ I ***gargle*** with salt water.　我用鹽水漱口。

♤ Actually, I take showers in the morning rather than baths in the evening.　事實上，我早上淋浴而不是晚上洗澡。

♤ It's healthy to ***soak*** in the bath tub.　泡在澡缸裡洗是有益健康的。

**——————————————

turn on 打開　　***a bit*** 稍微；一點

Washing Up ··

A : ***The water pressure is a bit low.*** 水壓低了一點。

B : That's because this is the peak use period.
　　因為現在是用水的尖峯時間。

A : When is the water pressure higher? 什麼時候水壓會比較高？

B : Around nine o'clock at night is better.
　　大約晚上九點時就比較好了。

＊　　　　　＊　　　　　＊

A : ***The water heater isn't working properly.***
　　熱水器故障了。

B : I know, a repairman is coming to fix it.
　　我知道，有個修理工人會來修理。

A : When will it get fixed? 何時才會修好呢？

B : The repairman should be here tomorrow.
　　工人明天才會來。

＊＊────────────────

　　repairman〔rɪˈpɛr͵mæn, -mən〕*n.* 修理工人

家庭小常識　工作一整天回來，腰酸背痛、全身疲勞，這時在溫水中加入少許的白醋或檸檬汁，然後沐浴，即可消除疲勞；刷牙後用檸檬汁擦拭牙齒，還可以潔白牙齒，鞏固牙床。

Warm-up

tile〔taɪl〕*n.* 磁磚	scrub〔skrʌb〕*v.* 刷洗
cleaner〔'klinɚ〕*n.* 清潔劑	mirror〔'mɪrɚ〕*n.* 鏡子

———————— ● 打掃浴室 ● ————————

♤ Use this rag to clean the ***tiles***.　　用這塊抹布擦淨磁磚。

♤ Who left the ring around the ***tub***?　　是誰把戒指忘在澡盆旁邊？

♤ I have to clean the bathroom at least once a week.　　我一週至少須清理浴室一次。

♤ You can use newspaper to clean off the ***mirror***.　　你可以用張報紙把鏡子擦乾淨。

♤ This glass ***cleaner*** will clean the mirror just fine.　　用這種玻璃清潔劑可以把玻璃擦得很乾淨。

♤ You'll have to ***scrub*** the tiles with an old toothbrush.　　你得用把舊牙刷刷一刷磁磚。

♤ This mirror always fogs up after I take a hot shower.　　每當我沖完熱水澡，鏡子總會變得霧氣濛濛。

**————————————————

　rag〔ræg〕*n.* 布片　　***fog up*** 起霧

Cleaning the Bathroom ·······································

A : This mirror needs cleaning. What should I use to clean it？這面鏡子需要擦了，我該用什麼擦呢？

B : ***You can use newspaper to clean off the mirror.***
你可以用報紙擦。

A : What kind of newspaper should I use？
用哪種報紙呢？

B : Business newspapers work the best.
用商業報紙最好擦。

　　　　　　＊　　　　　＊　　　　　＊

A : ***This mirror always fogs up after I take a hot shower.***
每當我沖完熱水澡，鏡子總會變得霧氣濛濛。

B : So how do you shave in the morning ?
那麼你早上如何刮鬍子呢？

A : I use old newspapers, then I can see myself clearly.
我用舊報紙擦鏡子，那樣我就可以看清楚自己的臉了。

B : Old newspapers. I'll have to remember that.
舊報紙！我得記下這一招。

＊＊─────────────────

shave〔ʃev〕*v.* 刮鬍子

Unit 8

The Laundry Room 洗衣室

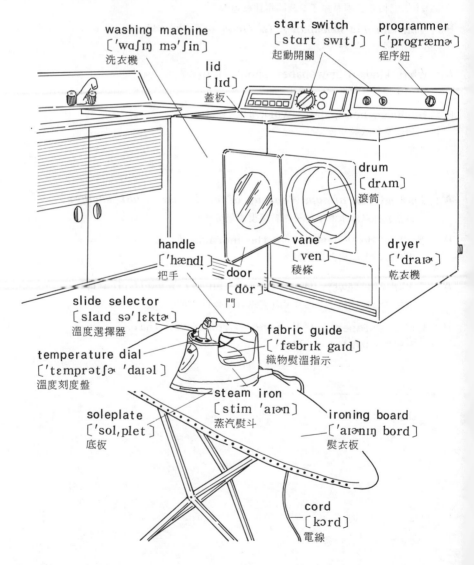

washing machine
〔'waʃɪŋ mə'ʃin〕
洗衣機

start switch
〔start swɪtʃ〕
起動開關

programmer
〔'progræmə〕
程序鈕

lid
〔lɪd〕
蓋板

drum
〔drʌm〕
滾筒

handle
〔'hændl〕
把手

vane
〔ven〕
稜條

dryer
〔'draɪə〕
乾衣機

door
〔dor〕
門

slide selector
〔slaɪd sə'lɛktə〕
溫度選擇器

fabric guide
〔'fæbrɪk gaɪd〕
織物熨溫指示

temperature dial
〔'tɛmprətʃə 'daɪəl〕
溫度刻度盤

steam iron
〔stim 'aɪən〕
蒸汽熨斗

soleplate
〔'sol,plet〕
底板

ironing board
〔'aɪənɪŋ bord〕
熨衣板

cord
〔kɔrd〕
電線

Warm-up

laundry〔'lɔndrɪ〕*n.* 洗衣(店)
laundry basket 洗衣籃
detergent〔dɪ'tɝdʒənt〕*n.* 洗劑
rinse〔rɪns〕*v.* 清洗
shrink〔ʃrɪŋk〕*v.* 縮水
spot〔spɑt〕*n.* 汚點
tag〔tæg〕*n.* 標籤
dryer〔'draɪɚ〕*n.* 烘乾機(= *drier*)
hang〔hæŋ〕*v.* 掛
laundromat〔'lɔndrəmæt,'lɑn-〕*n.* 自助洗衣店
clothespin〔'klozpɪn,'kloðz-〕*n.* 曬衣夾
clothesline〔'kloz,laɪn,'kloðz-〕*n.* 曬衣繩
pile up 堆積

do the laundry 洗衣
washing machine 洗衣機
load〔lod〕*n.* 洗一回的量
bleach〔blitʃ〕*v.* 漂白
resistant〔rɪ'zɪstənt〕*adj.* 有抵抗力的
laundry soap 洗衣皂
dry clean 乾洗
hanger〔'hæŋɚ〕*n.* 衣架

──────●洗　衣●──────

♧ Put your clothes in the ***laundry basket***.

把你的衣服放入洗衣籃內。

♧ I have to ***do the laundry*** because I don't have any clean clothes.

我得洗衣服了，因為已經沒有乾淨衣服穿了。

♧ Let's ***fill*** the ***washing machine***.

我們把衣服放入洗衣機裏吧!

♧ Add a cupful of ***detergent*** to the machine.

加一杯洗潔劑到洗衣機中。

**──────────────

cupful〔'kʌp,fʊl〕*n.* 一杯之量

♤ One cup is good for one *load*.　　洗一次用一杯最恰當。

♤ Next, *rinse* the clothes.　　接著是用水沖洗衣服。

♤ The whites need to be *bleached*.　　白色衣物需要漂白。

♤ Most of my clothes are *shrink resistant*.　　我大多數的衣服都不會縮水。

♤ The *spot* on this shirt won't come off.　　襯衫上的斑點洗不掉了。

♤ Can you run down to the store to get me some *laundry soap*?　　你能不能跑去商店幫我買洗衣皂？

♤ You've used too much detergent.　　你洗潔劑放太多了。

♤ The *tag* says "*dry clean only*".　　標籤上寫著:「只能乾洗」。

♤ I put the laundry in the *dryer*.　　我把衣物放進烘乾機。

♤ I'll *hang* the laundry *up* to dry.　　我要把衣物掛起來晾乾。

♤ The laundry has *piled up*.　　待洗衣物堆積如山。

Doing the Laundry ···

A : Where are you going now？ 你現在要上哪去？

B : To the laundromat. 去自助洗衣店。

A : At this hour？ 現在就去？

B : *I have to do the laundry because I don't have any clean clothes.* 我得現在去洗，因爲我已經沒牛件乾淨衣服穿了。

*　　　　　*　　　　　*

A : Should I wash this jacket in warm water or cold water？
   我該用溫水或是冷水洗這件夾克？

B : Neither. 都不行。

A : What do you mean？ 你說什麼？

B : *The tag says "dry clean only".*
   標籤上寫說，「只能乾洗」。

家庭小常識　衣服染到墨漬的話，一般洗衣粉是洗不掉的，要用阿摩尼亞水溶液浸泡三小時，再用手搓洗就能輕易去污。

Warm-up

iron ［'aɪən］ *v.* 熨衣服　*n.* 熨斗
ironing board　熨衣板　　steam iron 蒸汽熨斗
starch ［stɑrtʃ］ *n.* 漿糊　　stiff ［stɪf］ *adj.* 硬的
unplug ［ʌn'plʌg］*v.* 拔掉插頭　crease ［kris］ *v.* 變皺

● 熨衣服 ●

♠ Fold up the ***ironing board*** after using it.

熨衣板使用後要摺疊起來。

♠ Careful, the iron is hot.

小心點，熨斗很燙。

♠ My iron needs to be repaired.

我的熨斗需要修理。

♠ Do you have a ***steam iron***?

你有蒸汽熨斗嗎？

♠ Looks like I put too much ***starch*** on it.

我好像放太多漿糊了。

♠ ***Unplug*** the iron once you're done using it.

用完熨斗後，必須把插頭拔掉。

♠ This shirt feels a little bit ***stiff***.

這件襯衫穿起來有點硬。

♠ It's faster if you use a steam iron.

如果你使用蒸汽熨斗熨會快一些。

♠ I'm good at ***creasing*** pants.

我很容易把褲子弄皺。

**

fold up 摺疊

Ironing ···

A : ***Careful, the iron is hot.*** 小心，這熨斗很燙。

B : I know. 我知道。

A : And don't forget to unplug the iron once you're done using it. 不要忘了每次用完時，要拔掉熨斗的插頭。

B : Don't worry, I will. 別擔心，我會的。

*   *   *

A : ***Do you have a steam iron?*** 你有蒸汽熨斗嗎？

B : No, I just use this one. 沒有，我只用這一種。

A : It's faster if you use a steam iron.
   如果你用蒸汽熨斗的話會比較省時。

B : I know, but I like this one. 我知道，不過我喜歡用這一種。

家庭小常識　衣服上有污垢，千萬不可用熨斗去燙，否則，將永遠留有污垢的痕跡而洗不乾淨。

Unit 9

Recreation 娛樂

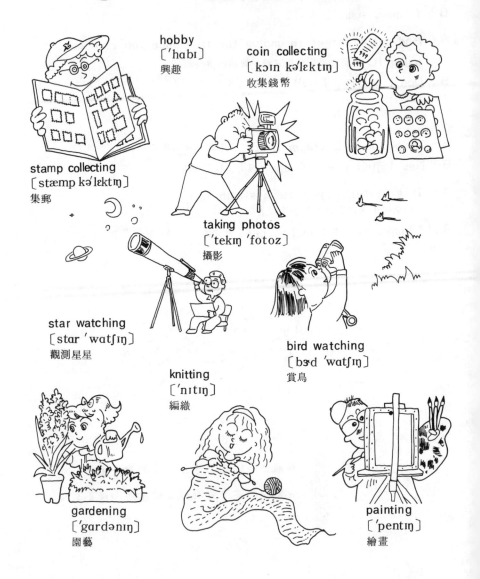

hobby
[ˈhɑbɪ]
興趣

stamp collecting
[stæmp kəˈlɛktɪŋ]
集郵

coin collecting
[kɔɪn kəˈlɛktɪŋ]
收集錢幣

taking photos
[ˈtekɪŋ ˈfotoz]
攝影

star watching
[stɑr ˈwɑtʃɪŋ]
觀測星星

bird watching
[bɝd ˈwɑtʃɪŋ]
賞鳥

knitting
[ˈnɪtɪŋ]
編織

gardening
[ˈgɑrdənɪŋ]
園藝

painting
[ˈpentɪŋ]
繪畫

Warm-up

video game 電動玩具　　　　laser printer 雷射印表機
memory〔ˈmɛmərɪ〕*n.* 記憶體　software〔ˈsɔft,wɛr〕*n.* 軟體
screen〔skrin〕*n.* 螢幕　　hardware〔ˈhɑrd,wɛr〕*n.* 硬體
PC（personal computer）個人電腦
compatible〔kəmˈpætəbl̩〕*adj.* 相容的
keyboard〔ˈki,bord〕*n.* 鍵盤　monitor〔ˈmɑnətɚ〕*n.* 螢幕

———————————● 電　腦 ●———————————

♤ Since we bought junior a computer, his grades have improved.

自從我們買電腦給小兒子之後，他的成績進步了。

♤ Don't just play *video games* all day! Do your homework!

別整天打電動玩具！去做功課！

♤ This computer is easy to use. We have one in school just like it.

這台電腦很容易操作，我們學校裏有一台同樣的。

♤ I'd like a *laser printer*, but I can't afford one.

我很想要一台雷射印表機，但是太貴了我買不起。

♤ Is your computer IBM *compatible*?

你的電腦跟 IBM 相容嗎？

**————————————————

junior〔ˈdʒunjɚ〕*n.* 年少者

♤ How much **memory** does your computer have?　　你的電腦記憶體有多大?

♤ What kind of **software** do you use?　　你使用哪一種軟體?

♤ I don't have a **PC**, but my friend lets me use his.　　我沒有個人電腦,不過我的朋友借我用他的。

♤ How much will it cost to upgrade the software?　　改善軟體品質要花多少錢?

♤ What's the difference between **hardware** and software?　　硬體跟軟體有什麼不同?

♤ What does megabyte mean?　　"megabyte"是什麼意思?

♤ What applications can I use this software for?　　我用這種軟體有何用途?

＊＊──────────

upgrade〔'ʌp'gred〕*v.* 改善
megabyte〔'mɛgə,baɪt〕*n.* 電腦記憶單位(約相當於 100 萬個 byte)
application〔,æplə'keʃən〕*n.* 用途

Computers ···

A : ***Don't just play video games all day*! *Do your homework*!**
別整天打電動玩具！去做功課！

B : But mom, I'm using this computer to do my homework.
但是，媽，我正在用電腦寫功課。

A : Oh yeah? Then why are there spaceships on the screen?
哦，真的嗎？那螢幕上為什麼有那些太空船？

B : OK mom, I'll do my homework in a couple of minutes.
好吧，媽，再幾分鐘我就去做功課了。

A : When I say do your homework, I mean right now!
我說要你去做功課，是要你馬上就去做！

*   *   *

A : ***Is your computer IBM compatible*?** 你的電腦跟IBM相容嗎？

B : Yes. It cost a little more but it's worth it.
是的，雖然貴了一點，不過很值得。

A : What kind of software do you use? 你使用哪種軟體？

B : The kind I use now is in both Chinese and English.
我現在用的是中英文兼俱的軟體。

*   *   *

A : Do you have a PC? 你有個人電腦嗎？

B : ***I don't have a PC, but my friend lets me use his.***
我沒有，不過我朋友借我用他的。

A : I heard that PCs are getting cheaper all the time.
聽說個人電腦一直在降價。

B : Actually I'm shopping around now.
事實上我正在四處比價蒐購。

Warm-up

drum〔drʌm〕*n.* 鼓

violin〔ˌvaɪə'lɪn〕*n.* 小提琴

cello〔'tʃɛlo〕*n.* 大提琴

flute〔flut〕*n.* 橫笛；長笛

concert hall 音樂廳

play〔ple〕*v.* 彈奏；敲打（樂器）

bass guitar〔bes gɪ'tɑr〕*n.* 低音吉他

saxophone〔'sæksə,fon〕*n.* 薩克斯風

piano〔pɪ'æno〕*n.* 鋼琴

trumpet〔'trʌmpɪt〕*n.* 喇叭

band〔bænd〕*n.* 樂團

oboe〔'obo〕*n.* 雙簧管

local〔'lokḷ〕*adj.* 當地的

pub〔pʌb〕*n.* 酒吧

───── ● 樂　器 ● ─────

♧ The neighbors will get mad if I practice **playing** my **drums** late at night.

如果我半夜練習打鼓的話，那些鄰居會發瘋。

♧ Can you play the **piano**?

你會彈鋼琴嗎？

♧ Our school **band** needs someone who can play the **trumpet**.

我們學校的樂隊需要會吹喇叭的人。

♧ They need someone who can play **bass guitar** to join their band.

他們樂團需要會彈低音吉他的人加入。

♧ A famous **saxophone** player will perform at the **concert hall** tonight.

今晚將有位聞名的薩克斯風演奏家在音樂廳演奏。

＊＊───────────────

bass〔bes〕*n.* 低音樂器

Musical Instruments ···

A : I heard they're playing at the local pub tonight.
聽說他們今晚會在本地的酒吧演奏。

B : **They need someone who can play bass guitar to join their band.** 他們樂團需要會彈低音吉他的人加入。

A : Really? I know someone who can play bass guitar.
眞的？我認識一位會彈低音吉他的人。

B : We can go to the pub tonight and talk to them before they start. 我們可以今晚到酒吧去，在演奏開始前和他們談一談。

*   *   *

A : **Can you play the piano?** 你會彈鋼琴嗎？

B : I used to play the piano well, but I haven't practiced recently. 以前彈得不錯，但最近很少練習了。

A : Why not? 爲什麼？

B : Too many exams. 考試太多了。

家庭小常識 口琴輕薄短小，是出外旅行助興的好伙伴，但吹過後，記得要用布把口琴抹淨，拍去口琴上的涎沫，然後收藏在盒子裏，以免塵埃飛入口琴內，減短口琴的壽命。

Warm-up

outside〔'aʊt'saɪd〕*adv.* 外面　exercise bicycle　健身車

exercise〔'ɛksə͵saɪz〕*v.* 運動　indoors〔'ɪn'dorz〕*adv.* 在屋內

inside〔'ɪn'saɪd〕*adv.* 在裏面　〔ɪn'saɪd〕*prep.* 在～裏面

basement〔'besmənt〕*n.* 地下室

────────── ● 室內遊戲 ● ──────────

♤ It's raining ***outside*** so we can only play cards now.

現在外面正在下雨，所以我們只能玩撲克牌。

♤ Don't run around ***inside*** the house！ You'll break something.

不要在房子裏跑來跑去，會把東西打破的。

♤ I have to ***exercise indoors*** when it's too cold outside.

外面天氣太冷時，我就必須在室內做運動。

♤ I bought this ***exercise bicycle*** for rainy days.

我買這輛健身車是爲了雨天時可以騎。

♤ The children can play in the ***basement***, it's big enough.

孩子們可以在地下室玩，那裏夠大。

♤ Let's play hide and go seek！

我們來玩捉迷藏吧！

────────────────────────

＊＊

hide and go seek 捉迷藏（＝*hide and seek*）

Indoor Games ··

A : I heard you race bicycles now.
聽說你現在參加自行車競賽。

B : That's right. Now I ride every day for training.
沒錯，現在我每天練習騎自行車。

A : What if it rains?
如果下雨怎麼辦？

B : ***I bought this exercise bicycle for rainy days.***
我買這輛健身車就是爲了下雨天時可以騎。

           *   *   *

A : It's raining outside. What can we do inside?
外面在下雨，我們在室內要做什麼？

B : How about playing cards? 打牌好不好？

A : No, I don't feel like playing cards.
不好，我不想打牌。

B : I know, ***let's play hide and go seek***!
知道了，我們來玩捉迷藏吧！

A : Yeah, that's a good idea!
好，眞是個好主意！

B : I'll count to a hundred. Ready?
我要數到一百，準備好了嗎？

---

race〔res〕*v.* 競賽   count〔kaʊnt〕*v.* 數

Warm-up

collect〔kəˈlɛkt〕v. 收集　　　coin〔kɔɪn〕n. 錢幣
sewing machine 縫紉機　　　　by hand 用手
baste〔best〕v. 假縫　　　　　hem〔hɛm〕n. 縫邊
alter〔ˈɔltə〕v. 改　　　　　　fanatic〔fəˈnætɪk〕n. 狂熱者
crochet〔kroˈʃe〕v. 用鈎針編織

──────● 嗜　好 ●──────

♤ Do you **collect baseball** cards? 你收集棒球卡片嗎？

♤ He's been all over the world, so he collects **coins**. 他遊遍全世界，所以他收集錢幣。

♠ I'm **crocheting** a piece for the table in the living room. 我正在用鈎針編織客廳飯桌用的桌巾。

♤ Use the **sewing machine**. Doing it **by hand** is too slow. 用縫紉機吧！用手縫太慢了。

♤ How do you like my crocheting? 你覺得我織得如何？

♤ I **basted** the **hem** last night. 我昨晚已以假縫固定布邊了。

♤ I would like to have this dress **altered**. 我要改這件洋裝。

♤ I don't collect stamps, but my older brother does. 我沒集郵，但我哥哥有。

♤ Do you want to see my stamp collection? 你想不想看看我收集的郵票？

Hobbies ···

A : This crochet rug is really nice. Is it hard to make?
　　這條針織的地毯眞的很不錯。很難織嗎？

B : No, not at all. I'll show you how to crochet.
　　不，一點也不難，我教你怎麽織。

A : Do you have anything to crochet now that I can help with?
　　旣然我會織了，你有什麽要我幫忙織的嗎？

B : Yes, *I'm crocheting a piece for the table in the living room*. 有，我正在織一條客廳飯桌用的桌巾。

　　　　　　*　　　　　*　　　　　*

A : *Do you collect baseball cards*? 你收集棒球卡片嗎？

B : No, but my younger brother does. He's a real baseball fanatic. 沒有，不過我弟弟有收集，他眞是個棒球迷。

✲✲————————————————

　　baseball card 棒球卡片

家庭小常識　用雙線縫衣服時，稍不留意，兩條線很容易糾結一處，但只要在兩線端分別打結，便不會有上述情況發生。

Warm-up

bookcase〔'bʊk,kes〕*n.* 書架　　lamp〔læmp〕*n.* 燈
personal〔'pɝsn̩l〕*adj.* 個人的　　arrange〔ə'rendʒ〕*v.* 排列
den〔dɛn〕*n.* 私室；私人書齋　　bookshelf〔'bʊk,ʃɛlf〕*n.* 書架

● 私人密室 ●

♤ This ***bookcase*** needs to be dusted.

這書架上的灰塵該清理了。

♤ That ***lamp*** needs a new light bulb.

那盞枱燈需要換個新的燈泡。

♤ I have to ***arrange*** the books on my desk.

我必須排一排我書桌上的書。

♤ Return the book to **its** **proper** place.

把書放回適當的位置。

♤ This is my ***personal*** library. I keep all my books here.

這是我私人的圖書室，我的藏書全部都放在這裏。

♤ I use a computer at the office and have another one here in the ***den***.

我在辦公室裏使用電腦，而我的書齋裏也有一台。

**

bulb〔bʌlb〕*n.* 電燈泡　　proper〔'prɑpɚ〕*adj.* 合適的

The Den ·······································

A : ***This is my personal library. I keep all my books here.***
　　這是我私人的圖書室，我的藏書全部都放在這裏。

B : How many books do you have?
　　你有多少本書？

A : About two hundred.
　　大約兩百本。

B : Who is your favorite writer?
　　你最喜歡的作家是哪一位？

A : I like the plays written by Shakespeare the best.
　　我最喜歡莎士比亞所寫的劇本。

　　　　　　　　*　　　　　　*　　　　　　*

A : Have you seen my comic book?
　　你有沒有看到我的漫畫書？

B : Which one?　哪一本？

A : My new "Ultra-Sonic Man" comic book. I left it on this
　　bookshelf.
　　我那本新的「超音速人」漫畫書，我先前放在這個書架上的。

B : Oh, that one. Joey is reading it now.
　　噢，是那本，喬伊正在看。

A : Tell him to ***return it to its proper place*** after he's done
　　with it.　叫他看完以後把它放回原位。

·

comic 〔'kɑmɪk〕 *n.* 漫畫（＝ *comic book*）
ultra 〔'ʌltrə〕 *adj.* 超過的　　sonic 〔'sɑnɪk〕 *adj.* 音速的

Unit 10

The Telephone 電話

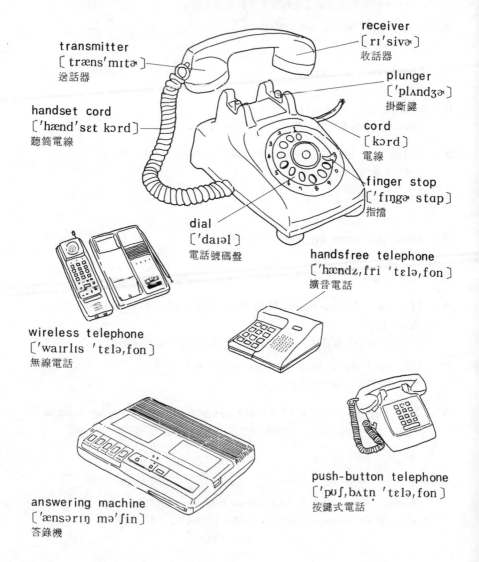

transmitter
〔træns'mɪtə〕
送話器

receiver
〔rɪ'sivə〕
收話器

plunger
〔'plʌndʒə〕
掛斷鍵

handset cord
〔'hænd'sɛt kɔrd〕
聽筒電線

cord
〔kɔrd〕
電線

finger stop
〔'fɪŋgə stɑp〕
指擋

dial
〔'daɪəl〕
電話號碼盤

handsfree telephone
〔'hændz,fri 'tɛlə,fon〕
擴音電話

wireless telephone
〔'waɪrlɪs 'tɛlə,fon〕
無線電話

answering machine
〔'ænsərɪŋ mə'ʃin〕
答錄機

push-button telephone
〔'pʊʃ,bʌtn 'tɛlə,fon〕
按鍵式電話

Warm-up

call sb. back 回電話   ring 〔rɪŋ〕 *v*. (電話)鈴響
answer 〔'ænsɚ〕 *v*. 回答；接(電話)
(This is~) speaking. 我是~。   hold on (電話)不掛斷
dial 〔'daɪəl〕 *v*. 撥電話   put through 接通；轉接
available 〔ə'veləbḷ〕 *adj*. 可得的；有空的

────────── ● 接電話 ● ──────────

♧ Shall I have her *call* you *back*?

要我叫她回電嗎？

♧ Please *answer* the phone.

請接一下電話。

♧ The telephone is *ringing*.

電話響了。

♧ Hello, *this is* George *speaking*.

喂，我是喬治。

♧ He's out at the moment.

他現在出去了。

♧ May I ask who's calling?

請問您哪裏找？

♧ I'll give you her telephone number. Could you call her there?

我告訴你她的電話號碼，請你打到那裏找她，好嗎？

♧ I'm afraid you have the wrong number.

你恐怕撥錯號碼了。

♤ Can you *hold on* a second?　　　等一會好嗎?

♤ I'm sorry, he just left.　　　很抱歉,他剛走。

♤ What number did you *dial*?　　　你打幾號?

♤ Where are you now?　　　你現在人在哪裏?

♤ He won't be back until next Monday.　　　他下禮拜一才會回來。

♤ Could you call again after 3 o'clock?　　　請你三點以後再打來好嗎?

♤ He is busy on another line.　　　他正在接另一個電話。

♤ I'll see if I can get him for you.　　　我看看能不能幫你找到他。

♤ Speaking. Who is this, please?　　　我就是,請問您是哪位?

♤ Hold on. I'll put you through now.　　　稍等,我立刻爲您轉接。

♤ He'll be with you in a moment.　　　他馬上過來。

♤ I'm sorry to have kept you waiting.　　　抱歉讓您久等。

♤ She's on the phone right now.　　　她現在正在講電話。

♤ She's not available now.　　　她現在沒空。

Receiving Calls ····································

A : ***May I ask who is calling*** ? 請問您哪裏找？

B : This is Ronald. 我是羅納德。

A : Shall I have her call you back ? 要我叫她回電嗎？

B : Yes, please do. 是的，麻煩你了。

*   *   *

A : Is this Joey's Fried Chicken ? 是喬伊炸雞店嗎？

B : No, ***I'm afraid that you have the wrong number.***
    不是，你恐怕打錯了。

A : Oh, I'm sorry. 噢，眞是抱歉。.

B : No problem. 沒關係。

*   *   *

A : ***Where are you now*** ? 你現在人在哪裏？

B : I'm at the international airport. 我在國際機場。

A : Just stay right there. I'll have someone meet you there.
    就在那裏等，我會找人去接你。

家庭小常識　電話使用頻繁，你可曾注意過電話的清潔？清潔電話時，必須使用含有甘油酯的清潔劑或酒精擦拭；號碼盤的部分可以用筷子或原子筆包上抹布擦拭。

Warm-up

get hold of 與～取得聯繫   cancel 〔'kænsl〕 *v.* 取消
reserve 〔rɪ'zɝv〕 *v.* 預訂   reservation 〔,rɛzə'veʃən〕 *n.* 預約
return 〔rɪ'tɝn〕 *v.* 回覆（電話）
disturb 〔dɪ'stɝb〕 *v.* 打擾   This is ～ calling. 我是～。
regards 〔rɪ'gɑrdz〕 *n. pl.* 問候   give sb. a ring 打電話給某人
extension 〔ɪk'stɛnʃən〕 *n.* 分機

● 打電話 ●

♤ I'd like to make an appointment with the doctor.
我想和醫生約時間見面。

♤ I'm so glad to *get hold of* you
at last.
真高興，我終於找到你了。

♤ I'd like to *reserve* a room.
我想預訂房間。

♤ I'd like to *cancel* my *reservation*.
我想取消預約。

♤ I'm sorry I couldn't *return*
your call last night.
很抱歉我昨晚没能回你的電
話。

♤ Sorry to *disturb* you so late
at night.
很抱歉，這麼晚了還打擾你。

** ————————————————————

appointment 〔ə'pɔɪntmənt〕 *n.* 約會

♤ I'm calling you from a book-
store.

我在一家書店裏打電話給你。

♤ *This is* Dan *calling*.

我是丹。

♤ Please say hello to everyone
for me.

請代我向大家問好。

♤ Please give my *regards* to
your boss.

請代我問候你們老板。

♤ Can you tell me how to get
to your office?

你能不能告訴我貴公司該怎
麼去呢?

♤ Do you know what time he'll
be in?

你知道他何時回來嗎?

♤ Hello, could I speak to Mr.
Lee?

喂,我找李先生。

♤ Will you please ask him to
call me back?

請你叫他回我電話好嗎?

♤ Could you put me through to
Mr. Lee, please?

請你幫我轉接李先生好嗎?

♤ I'll *give* you *a ring* again later.

我晚一點再打給你。

♤ Would you connect me with
extension 308?

請你幫我轉三〇八分機好嗎?

Making Calls ···

A : Hello, Grand Hotel. May I help you?
喂，圓山飯店，能爲您效勞嗎？

B : *Yes, I'd like to reserve a room.* 是的，我想預訂房間。

A : When would you like to reserve it? 您想訂什麽時候的房間呢？

B : Tomorrow evening. 明天晚上。

A : What kind of room? 哪種房間？

B : A single room. 單人房。

*　　　　　*　　　　　*

A : It's good to hear from you again.
眞高興接到你的電話。

B : *I'm sorry I couldn't return your call last night.*
很抱歉，我昨晚沒法回你的電話。

A : So how was your trip to Bermuda? 那你的百慕達之旅如何呀？

B : It was very nice there. 那地方實在不錯。

*　　　　　*　　　　　*

A : Hello, is Mr. Jones there? 喂，瓊斯先生在嗎？

B : No, he's not here right now. 不，他現在不在。

A : *Do you know what time he'll be in?*
你知道他什麽時候回來嗎？

B : He should be back by seven o'clock this evening.
今天晚上七點以前會回來。

Bermuda 〔bəˊmjudə〕 *n.* 百慕達群島

Warm-up

leave 〔liv〕 v. 留下　　　　　　message 〔'mɛsɪdʒ〕 n. 留言
reach 〔ritʃ〕 v. (以電話等) 連絡
as soon as 一～就…　　　　　spell 〔spɛl〕 v. 拼 (字)
write down 寫下來

—————● 電話留言 ●—————

♤ Would you like to *leave* a *message*? 您想留言嗎?

♤ Can I take a message? 您要留言嗎?

♤ Would you like me to have him call you? 您要我叫他回電嗎?

♤ Where can he *reach* you? 他在哪裏可以連絡上您?

♤ Can I have your name and number? 能否告訴我您的姓名和電話?

♤ Shall I have him call you back later? 要不要我叫他待會回您電話?

♤ I'll have him call you *as soon as* he gets back. 他回來後,我會告訴他儘快打電話給您。

♤ Does he know your number? 他知道您的電話號碼嗎?

♤ I'll give him your message. 我會告訴他您的留言。

♤ Can you *spell* that for me? 能不能麻煩您把字拼出來?

♤ I'll tell her you called once she gets back. 她一回來我就告訴她說你打過電話來。

♤ Let me *write* that *down*. 先讓我寫下來。

Taking Messages ·······················

A : **Would you like to leave a message?**
　　您想留言嗎?

B : Yes, please. Tell him that Mr. Jackson called.
　　是的。告訴他傑克森先生打過電話來。

A : Does he know your number? 他知道您的電話號碼嗎?

B : Yes, he does. 是的,他知道。

　　　　　　　*　　　　　　*　　　　　　*

A : I'm afraid that she's not here right now.
　　抱歉她現在不在這裏。

B : It's urgent. 我有要緊的事找她。

A : In that case, **I'll tell her you called once she gets back.**
　　那樣的話,她一回來我會立刻告訴她你打過電話來。

---

　　urgent〔'ɝdʒənt〕*adj.* 緊急的
　　in that case 那樣的話

Warm-up

overseas〔'ovɚ'siz〕*adj.*海外的　　person-to-person直接叫人的
collect call 對方付費的電話　　operator〔'ɑpə,retɚ〕*n.*接線生
echo〔'ɛko〕*n.* 回音　　special rate 特別優待；特價時段
time difference 時差　　station-to-station 叫號的
charge〔tʃɑrdʒ〕*v.* 索價；記帳

●打長途電話●

♤ I'd like to make an *overseas* call to Vienna, Austria.

我想打一通國際電話到奧地利的維也納。

♤ I'd like to make a *person-to-person* call.

我想打一通叫人電話。

♤ The number is 1-638-382-1823.

電話號碼是1-638-382-1823。

♤ I'm calling from the United States.

我是從美國打來的。

♤ I'd like to make a *collect call* to France.

我想打一通對方付費電話到法國。

＊＊

Vienna〔vɪ'ɛnə〕*n.* 維也納
Austria〔'ɔstrɪə〕*n.* 奧地利

♤ What time is it there now? 　　那裏現在是幾點？

♤ *Operator*, there was an *echo* 　接線生，電話有回音，所以
and I couldn't hear well. 　　我聽不太清楚。

♤ Will you put me through 　　請再幫我接通一次好嗎？
again?

♤ At what time do your *special* 　你們特價是由何時開始？
rates start?

♤ What's the *time difference* 　台北和羅馬的時差是多久？
between Taipei and Rome?

♤ Can you *charge* the call to my 　你能不能把電話費記在我信
credit card number? 　　用卡的帳上？

♤ It's cheaper if you dial direct. 　你直撥比較便宜。

♤ There's too much static. I 　　干擾太多了，我聽不清楚。
couldn't hear clearly.

♤ I'd like to make a *station-to-* 　我想打一通叫號電話。
station call.

♤ Operator, could you tell me the 　接線生，你能不能告訴我加
country code of Canada? 　　拿大的國碼？

♤ How much will it cost to make a 　打到香港的電話三分鐘要多
three minutes' call to Hong Kong? 　少錢？

＊＊──────────────────

direct 〔də'rɛkt, daɪ-〕*adv.* 直接地
static 〔'stætɪk〕*n.* 干擾　　*country code* 國碼

Calling Long Distance ·······································

A : **Where are you calling from**? 你這電話從哪裏打來的?

B : I'm calling from the United States.
   我從美國打來的。

A : What time is it there now? 美國現在幾點?

B : It's midnight here so it's cheaper to call.
   現在是半夜,所以電話費比較便宜。

* * *

A : **Operator, I'd like to make an overseas call to Vienna, Austria.**
   接線生,我想打一通國際電話到奧地利的維也納。

B : Would you like to use a credit card?
   您想用信用卡付費嗎?

A : Yes, I would. 是的。

B : What is your credit card number?
   您的信用卡號碼是幾號?

* * *

A : Operator, the line just got cut off. **Will you put me through to the same number again**?
   接線生,我的電話剛被切斷了。請再幫我打一次相同號碼好嗎?

B : Sure. I'll get back to you when the line gets through.
   當然,電話一接通,我就會回電給您。

A : Thank you. 謝謝。

Warm-up

tone〔ton〕*n.* 聲音　　　　　manage〔'mænɪdʒ〕*v.* 處理
fax〔fæks〕*v., n.* 傳眞　　　fax machine 傳眞機
garble〔'gɑrbl〕*v.* (傳眞)電文模糊不清

● 傳眞機・答錄機 ●

♤ At the sound of the ***tone*** please leave your name, number and message.

聽見聲響後，請留下您的姓名、電話及留言。

♤ ***Send***ing a ***fax*** message overseas is cheaper than calling.

以傳眞傳遞訊息至國外比打電話便宜。

♤ Every modern office should have a ***fax machine***.

現代化的辦公室都該備有一台傳眞機。

♤ Now that we have a fax machine we don't get many letters.

自從我們買了傳眞機以後，信件就不多了。

♤ Having a fax machine sure is convenient.

擁有傳眞機的確很方便。

♤ I will fax it.

我會以傳眞方式送過去。

♤ Thank you for your faxed letter of November 17.

謝謝您十一月十七日傳過來的傳眞信函。

♤ This fax message is ***garbled***, I can hardly read it.

這份傳眞電文很模糊，我幾乎看不出寫什麼。

Faxes, Answering Machine ················

A : *At the sound of the tone please leave your name, number and message.*

　　聽見聲響後，請留下您的姓名、電話及留言。

B : This is Mary, remember? The waitress at Bob's Burgers. Call me back.

　　我是瑪莉，記得嗎？就是那位鮑伯漢堡店的女服務生，回來打通電話給我。

＊　　　　＊　　　　＊

A : *Every modern office should have a fax machine.*

　　每個現代化辦公室都該有傳眞機。

B : That's true. I don't know how we would manage without ours. 沒錯。我很難想像沒有傳眞機我們該怎麼辦。

A : If you write a letter it takes at least a week.

　　如果是寫信，至少一個星期後，對方才能收到。

B : But sending a fax message only takes a few seconds.

　　但是傳眞一次，却只要幾秒鐘就可以了。

＊　　　　＊　　　　＊

A : *This fax message is garbled, I can hardly read it.*

　　這份傳眞電文很模糊，我幾乎看不出寫什麼。

B : It's the machine : we're getting a new one next week.

　　是傳眞機出毛病，我們下星期要再買一台新的。

A : It's really hard to do business without a good fax machine.

　　沒有好的傳眞機，眞的很難辦事。

Unit 11

Visitors 訪客

welcome
〔'wɛlkəm〕
歡迎

hostess
〔'hostɪs〕
女主人

guest
〔gɛst〕
客人

serve
〔sɝv〕
招待

host
〔host〕
主人

entertain
〔,ɛntɚ'ten〕
娛樂

chat with friends
〔tʃæt wɪð frɛndz〕
與朋友聊天

Warm-up

greet〔grit〕*v.* 迎接	ring〔rɪŋ〕*v.* 按（門鈴）
take the time 特地(花時間)	It's kind of you to … 你真好～
knock on 敲門	take off 脫下
Make yourself at home. 請勿拘禮。	
put on 穿上	slippers〔'slɪpəz〕*n.pl.* 拖鞋
let sb. in 請某人進入	Long time no see! 好久不見！
Come on in. 請進！	help yourself 自由取用

———————— ● 迎接客人 ● ————————

♤ I'd better go **greet** the guests. 我最好去迎接客人。

♤ Did someone just **ring** the doorbell? 有人剛剛按了門鈴嗎？

♤ Thank you for **taking the time** to come. 謝謝你特地前來。

♤ **It's kind of you to** come over. 您能來真是太好了。

♤ I'm glad that you came. 真高興你來了。

♤ Someone is **knock**ing **on** the door. 有人在敲門。

♤ Can you see who it is at the door ?　你能不能去看看門外是誰 ?

♤ Hello, we've been expecting you.　嗨，我們等你好久了 !

♤ Did you have trouble finding our house ?　我們家好找嗎 ?

♤ May I take your coat ?　我幫你拿外套好嗎 ?

♤ Would you like something to drink ?　你想喝點什麼嗎 ?

♤ *Make yourself at home*.　請不要太拘束 。

♤ Please come in.　請進 。

♤ Please *take off* your shoes.　請脫鞋 。

♤ Please *pul on* these *slippers*.　請穿拖鞋 。

♤ This is our place. We hope you like it.　這是我們住的地方，希望你喜歡 。

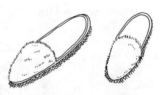

Welcoming Guests..

A : **Someone is knocking on the door.**
　　有人在敲門。

B : Can you see who it is ? 你能不能去看看是誰來了?

A : It's the Wilsons. 是威爾森一家人。

B : Please let them in. I invited them over to play bridge.
　　麻煩你去請他們進來,是我邀請他們過來打橋牌的。

　　　　　　＊　　　　　＊　　　　　＊

A : Hey Fred! Long time no see! Come on in.
　　嗨!佛瑞德!好久不見!快請進!

B : It has been a long time, hasn't it? 好久不見了,不是嗎?

A : That's right. **Make yourself at home.**
　　沒錯。請不要太拘束,就當在自己家裏一樣。

B : Thanks. Can I get a beer out of the fridge?
　　謝謝。我可以去冰箱拿罐啤酒喝嗎?

A : Sure, help yourself. 當然可以,請便。

＊＊ ─────────────────

fridge〔frɪdʒ〕*n.* 冰箱

家庭小常識　宴客後,屋內常會留有一股香煙的怪味
　　　　　　驅之不去,這時若在室內角落處放一隻
　　　　　　盛醋的碗,就可以把煙味除掉。

Warm-up

helping 〔'hɛlpɪŋ〕 *n.* （食物的）一份；一客
tray 〔tre〕 *n.* 盤子　　　　How about …? 要不要～?
Would you like …? 要不要～?　　pastry 〔'pestrɪ〕 *n.* 點心
homemade 〔'hom'med〕 *adj.* 自製的

● 招待客人 ●

♤ Won't you have some cake?　　　要不要吃點蛋糕?

♤ Pardon me, I have to wash　　　對不起，我得去洗個手。
my hands.

♤ Would you like another **help-**　　需要再來一份嗎?
ing?

♤ Would you like some chicken?　　要不要吃雞肉?

♤ I hope you like Chinese food.　　希望你喜歡中國菜。

♤ Always serve guests with a　　　送食物給客人時一定要用個
tray.　　　　　　　　　　　　盤子裝。

♤ **How about** another glass of　　要不要再來杯啤酒?
beer?

**

pardon 〔'pardn̩〕 *v.* 原諒

♤ Some more crackers?　　　　　要不要再吃些餅乾？

♤ How do you like your coffee?　　咖啡味道如何呢？

♤ If you want more, please help
　yourself.　　　　　　　　　　如果還要的話，請自行取用。

♤ Do try some of my *homemade*
　bread.　　　　　　　　　　　你一定要嚐嚐看我自己做的
　　　　　　　　　　　　　　　　麵包。

♤ Help yourself to whatever you
　can find in the refrigerator.　　冰箱裏的東西，要吃就自己
　　　　　　　　　　　　　　　　拿。

♤ Would you like coffee or tea?　　要喝咖啡還是茶？

♤ How about some *pastries*?　　　要不要吃些點心？

----

cracker〔'krækɚ〕*n.* 餅乾
refrigerator〔rɪ'frɪdʒəˌretɚ〕*n.* 冰箱

Serving Guests ··

A : That steak really tasted good. 牛排眞好吃。

B : ***Won't you have some cake***？要不要吃點蛋糕？

A : Well, just one slice, thank you. 嗯，一片就好，謝謝。

B : It's my own recipe. I hope you'll like it.
    這是我自己做的，希望你會喜歡。

A : Why, it's delicious！I must have that recipe.
    眞是太好吃了！我一定要學會怎麼做。

                    ＊   ＊   ＊

A : ***Would you like coffee or tea***？要喝咖啡還是茶？

B : Coffee, please.   咖啡。

A : How about some pastries with your coffee？
    要不要吃點糕餅配咖啡呢？

B : Yes, please. 好的，麻煩你。

                    ＊   ＊   ＊

A : Your ham and eggs are really delicious.
    你做的火腿蛋眞好吃。

B : ***Do try some of my homemade bread***. It makes very good
    toast. 你一定要嚐嚐看我自己做的麵包，烤過會非常好吃。

A : OK, I'll have two slices please.
    好的，請給我兩片。

---

recipe〔'rɛsəpɪ〕*n.*（食物的）烹調法
toast〔tost〕*n.* 烤麵包

Warm-up

entrance 〔'ɛntrəns〕 *n.* 門口   hall 〔hɔl〕 *n.* 大廳
to the right /left 向右/左轉   central air conditioning 中央空調
view 〔vju〕 *n.* 視野；景觀   balcony 〔'bælkənɪ〕 *n.* 陽台
repaint 〔ri'pent〕 *v.* 再油漆   switch 〔swɪtʃ〕 *n.* 開關
brand-new 〔'brænd'nju, -'nu〕 *adj.* 全新的
furniture 〔'fɝnɪtʃɚ〕 *n.* 傢俱   rattan 〔ræ'tæn〕 *n.* 籐

————● 帶客人參觀室內 ●————

♤ I got this drip-coffee maker for Christmas.　　這台滴泡咖啡壺是我聖誕節時收到的禮物。

♤ This is the *entrance hall*.　　這裏是大廳。

♤ The room *to the right* is the kitchen.　　右邊那間是廚房。

♤ We have *central air conditioning*.　　我們有中央空調。

♤ This is the living room.　　這裏是客廳。

♤ We have a beautiful *view* of the bay from our *balcony*.　　從陽台望出去，能看見海灣美麗的風景。

♤ We just had the house *repainted*.　　我們剛重新粉刷過房子。

♤ The light *switch* is over there.　　電燈的開關在那裏。

♤ Our washing machine is *brand-new*.　　我們的洗衣機是全新的。

♤ How do you like our new *furniture*?　　你覺得我們的新傢俱如何？

**————————————

drip 〔drɪp〕 *v.* 滴　　　bay 〔be〕 *n.* 海灣

Showing Guests Around ······································

A : How is the coffee? 咖啡的味道如何?

B : It's very good. 非常香醇。

A : *I got this drip-coffee maker for Christmas.*
   這台滴泡咖啡壺是我聖誕節時收到的禮物。

B : It sure makes good coffee.
   由它泡出來的咖啡眞的很好喝。

*　　　　　*　　　　　*

A : *How do you like our new furniture?*
   你覺得我們的新傢俱如何呢?

B : The furniture is sure nice. What is it made of?
   眞的很不錯,是用哪種材質做的呢?

A : It's rattan furniture, from the Philippines.
   這是從菲律賓進口的藤製傢俱。

**————————————————

Philippines〔'fɪlə,pinz〕*n.* 菲律賓群島

Warm-up

See you again. 再見。　Take care. 保重
pay sb. a visit 去拜訪某人　company〔'kʌmpənɪ〕*n.* 作伴
stop by 順道拜訪

— ● 送 客 ● —

♤ Why don't you stay until the rain stops?	你何不等雨停了再走？
♤ Why don't you stay for the night?	你何不在這裏過夜？
♤ *See you again.*	再見！
♤ My father will take you to the station.	家父會送你到車站。
♤ *Take care.*	保重！
♤ Please stay longer.	請待久一點。
♤ Come visit us again.	要再來拜訪我們哦！
♤ Thank you very much for *paying us a visit.*	非常謝謝你來拜訪我們。
♤ I hope that you will come more often.	希望你以後更常來。
♤ You can come visit us anytime.	你可以隨時來找我們。
♤ We certainly enjoyed your *company.*	和你在一起,我們十分愉快。
♤ We enjoyed having you with us.	和你在一起,我們十分愉快。

**——————————————

anytime〔'ɛnɪˌtaɪm〕*adv.* 隨時地

Sending off Departing Guests ··························

A : It's been nice to see all of you again.
　　能再見到你們，眞是太好了。

B : ***Come visit us again.*** 一定要再來哦！

A : I'll stop by the next time I'm in town.
　　下次我到鎭上來時，一定順道來拜訪。

B : We'll see you then. Have a good trip.
　　那時候再見！祝你一路順風！

*　　　　　*　　　　　*

A : ***Thank you very much for paying us a visit.***
　　非常謝謝你來拜訪我們。

B : It was my pleasure. 這是我的榮幸。

*　　　　　*　　　　　*

A : Well, thank you for your hospitality. We really enjoyed
　　our stay here. 謝謝你們的款待，在這裏眞是愉快極了！

B : ***We enjoyed having you with us, too. We hope you come
　　over more often.***
　　　　和你們在一起，我們也很愉快。希望你們以後更常來。

A : We definitely will. Well, so long.
　　　我們一定會的，再見。

B : Take care. 保重。

＊＊────────────────────

hospitality〔͵hɑspɪ'tælətɪ〕*n.* 殷勤款待

Warm-up

No thanks. 不，謝了。   donate〔'donet〕 *v.* 捐贈

May I help you? 我能幫你嗎？

───────● 不速之客 ●───────

♤ Would you be kind enough to come back later?	能不能請您待會再來？
♤ **No thanks**. I'm not interested.	不，謝了。我沒興趣。
♤ No thanks. I just bought some a few days ago.	不，謝了。我前幾天才剛買。
♤ I've already **donated**.	我已經捐了。
♤ I donate only to certain charity organizations.	我只捐給特定的慈善機構。
♤ I'm sorry, I'm too busy now.	很抱歉，我現在太忙了。
♤ Could you come back some other time?	以後再來，好嗎？
♤ Sorry, I already donated at the office.	很抱歉，我在辦公室已經捐過了。

**──────────────────────

charity〔'tʃærətɪ〕 *n.* 慈善

organization〔,ɔrgənə'zeʃən〕 *n.* 機構

Unwanted Visitors ························

A : Is Maria here right now? 瑪莉亞現在在嗎?

B : No, she's not here. *Would you be kind enough to come back later*?

不,她不在。你待會再來好嗎?

A : But she's never here! 可是她老是不在。

B : Maybe next time. 也許下次會在吧。

　　　　　　*　　　　　　*　　　　　　*

A : May I help you? 能為你效勞嗎?

B : Yes, we're on a mission from God to save the world.

是的,我們正肩負著上帝授與的使命,要拯救全世界。

A : *Sorry, I already donated at the office.*

很抱歉,在辦公室時我已經捐獻過了。

B : But the world is coming to an end!

但是世界末日就快來臨了!

A : Maybe you're right. Have a nice day.

或許你說的沒錯,再見。

---

mission〔'mɪʃən〕*n.* 使命

Have a nice day!「祝你有個美好的一天!」,原為離別時的祝福語,但在本篇對話中則帶有反諷意味,一方面表示不願再繼續這個談話,另一方面則反諷對方所言的「世界末日即將來臨」。可以簡單地譯為「再見吧!」。

Warm-up

next-door 鄰家的	out of order 故障
run out of 用光	chat 〔tʃæt〕 *v.* 聊天
portable 〔'portəbḷ, 'pɔr-〕 *adj.* 可攜帶的	

————————● 鄰　居 ●————————

♧ Why don't you come over and
have a cup of coffee?

你要不要過來喝杯咖啡？

♧ Hello, I'm Mary Lee. I just
moved in next door.

哈囉，我是李瑪莉，我剛搬
來隔壁。

♧ I'm your **next-door** neighbor.

我是你隔壁的鄰居。

♧ May I use your telephone?
Mine is **out of order**.

可以借用一下你的電話嗎？
我的電話故障了。

♧ I'm **running out of** sugar.
May I borrow a cup?

我的糖快用完了，可以借我
一杯糖嗎？

♧ May I borrow your lawn
mower? Mine hasn't arrived
yet.

可不可以借用一下你們的割
草機？我的還沒送到。

♤ Can you make your dog stop barking? We can't sleep.

你能不能讓你的狗不要再吠叫？我們都沒辦法睡覺。

♤ Please come over when you have the time.

有空時請過來坐坐。

♤ It's late. Can you keep the noise down?

已經很晚了。你能不能把音量放低一點？

♤ Can you turn down the stereo a little?

可不可以把音響關小聲一點呢？

♤ Thank you for watching the house while we were away.

我們不在的時候，謝謝你幫我們看家。

♤ When you have the time, please come over for a *chat*.

有空請過來聊一聊。

♤ You should have dinner with us sometime.

找個時間我們吃個飯。

♤ Is this your baseball? I found it in our back yard.

這是不是你的棒球？我在我們家後院撿到的。

♤ So you're the ones who just moved in. How do you like the neighborhood?

原來剛搬進來的就是你們。你們覺得這附近如何？

＊＊────────

turn down 轉小（收音機等的）聲音
neighborhood〔'nebɚ,hʊd〕*n.* 附近；鄰近

Neighbors ···

A : **Hello, I'm Mary Lee. I just moved in next door.**
　　哈囉，我是李瑪莉，剛搬來你們家隔壁。

B : Oh, you're the ones with the moving truck outside.
　　噢，外面那輛搬運卡車就是你們的。

A : That's right. We just arrived from Taiwan.
　　沒錯，我們剛從台灣搬來。

B : So, how do you like it here？ 嗯，你們覺得這裏如何呢？

A : It's kind of quaint. 非常新奇有趣。

　　　　　　＊　　　　　　＊　　　　　　＊

A : **May I use your telephone？ Mine is out of order.**
　　可不可以借用一下電話？我的故障了。

B : After the storm, mine's out of order too.
　　暴風雨過後，我的電話也故障了。

A : Oh no！ 噢！真糟糕！

B : I've got a portable phone. You can use it.
　　我有台行動電話，可以借你打。

A : Thanks. 謝謝。

＊＊────────────────────

　　quaint〔kwent〕*adj.* 新奇有趣的

Warm-up

lineman 〔'laɪnmən〕 *n.* 架線工人

electric meter 電錶　　　　water meter 水錶

copy 〔'kɑpɪ〕 *n.* 一份；一本　　send 〔sɛnd〕 *v.* 寄送

cancel 〔'kænsḷ〕 *v.* 取消　　　tip 〔tɪp〕 *n.* 小費

subscription 〔səb'skrɪpʃən〕 *n.* 訂閱

delivery person 送貨員　　　　gas bill 瓦斯費帳單

shut off 停閉(水、電、煤氣等)　turn off 關掉

electricity 〔ɪ,lɛk'trɪsətɪ,ə-〕 *n.* 電力

let sb. in 讓某人進來

● 送遞・水電維修 ●

♤ The *lineman* is checking our *electric meter*.

架線工人正在檢查我們的電錶。

♤ The man is here to look at the *water meter*.

那個人是來檢查水錶的。

♤ Here's the payment for this month's *deliveries*.

這是這個月送遞的費用。

♤ Do I pay in advance or at the end of the month?

我是該月初付，還是月底付呢？

**
---

payment 〔'pemənt〕 *n.* 支付之款

♤ I didn't get last month's *copy*. Can you *send* another one?

我沒拿到上個月的那一本。你能再寄一本給我嗎？

♤ I'd like to *cancel* my *subscription*.

我想取消訂閱。

♤ We can take comfort in knowing that the Police are here.

警方在這裏讓我們覺得很安慰。

♤ Here's a small *tip* for you.

這是給你的一點小費。

♤ The pizza *delivery person* is here.

送披薩的人在這裏。

♤ You better call the Police right away!

你最好馬上通知警方。

♤ Pay your *gas bill* before they *shut* it *off*.

在瓦斯還沒被停止供應之前，趕快去繳費吧。

♤ You had better pay the bill before they *turn off* your *electricity*.

你最好在被停止供電之前去繳費。

※※─ ──────────

take comfort 得到安慰

Deliveries, House Maintenance ·····························

A : Dad, **the man is here to look at our water meter**.
爸，查看水錶的人來了。

B : Let him in. The meter is in the basement. 請他進來,水錶在地下室。

A : Come on in, mister. My dad says it's in the basement.
請進，先生。我爸爸說水錶在地下室。

B : Thank you. 謝謝。

              *   *   *

A : Hello, Daily News ? **I'd like to cancel my subscription**.
哈囉，是「每日新聞」嗎？我想取消訂閱。

B : Sir, may I ask why you wish to cancel ? 先生，請問您為什麼要取消呢?

A : Because they don't have George the Cat cartoons anymore.
因為上面沒有喬治貓漫畫了。

B : I will inform the management, sir. 我會通知管理部門,先生。

              *   *   *

A : Oh no, we got another nasty letter from the Gas Company.
噢，糟糕，我們又收到瓦斯公司討厭的信了。

B : What for ? 怎麼說呢？

A : We haven't paid our gas bill for two months.
我們兩個月沒付瓦斯費了。

B : **You'd better pay your gas bill before they shut it off**.
你最好趁他們還沒停止供應瓦斯之前趕快繳費。

A : You're right. I'll go to their office and pay the bill today.
沒錯，今天我就去他們的辦公室繳費。

---

basement 〔'besmənt〕 *n.* 地下室   cartoon 〔kɑr'tun〕 *n.* 漫畫
inform 〔ɪn'fɔrm〕 *v.* 通知   management 〔'mænɪdʒmənt〕 *n.* 管理人員
nasty 〔'næstɪ〕 *adj.* 討厭的

Unit 12

Illness 生病

animal doctor
〔'ænəmḷ 'dɑktə〕
獸醫

surgeon
〔'sɝdʒən〕
外科醫生

medical technician
〔'mɛdɪkḷ tɛk'nɪʃən〕
醫技師

pediatrician
〔͵pidɪə'trɪʃən〕
小兒科醫生

hospital
〔'hɑspɪtḷ〕
醫院

doctor
〔'dɑktə〕
醫生

dentist
〔'dɛntɪst〕
牙醫

patient
〔'peʃənt〕
病人

bone fracture
〔bon 'fræktʃə〕
骨折

physician
〔fə'zɪʃən〕
內科醫生

nurse
〔nɝs〕
護士

Warm-up

under the weather 身體不適	faint〔fent〕*adj.* 暈眩的
in a daze 頭昏眼花	period〔'pɪrɪəd〕*n.* 生理期
cramps〔kræmps〕*n. pl.* 劇痛	fever〔'fivɚ〕*n.* 發燒
slight〔slaɪt〕*adj.* 輕微的	feverish〔'fivərɪʃ〕*adj.* 發燒的
sharp〔ʃɑrp〕*adj.* 劇烈的	pain〔pen〕*n.* 疼痛
dull〔dʌl〕*adj.* 不太感覺得到的	throbbing〔'θrɑbɪŋ〕*adj.* 震顫的
chill〔tʃɪl〕*n.* 寒慄	running nose 流鼻水
bleed〔blid〕*v.* 流血	stuffy〔'stʌfɪ〕*adj.* 阻塞的
uncomfortable〔ʌn'kʌmfətəbl̩〕*adj.* 不舒服的	
sneeze〔sniz〕*v.* 打噴嚏	cough〔kɔf〕*v.* 咳嗽
phlegm〔flɛm〕*n.* 痰	headache〔'hɛd,ek〕*n.* 頭痛
sore throat 喉嚨痛	hurt〔hɝt〕*v.* 痛
palpitate〔'pælpə,tet〕*v.* 急速地跳動	
breath〔brɛθ〕*n.* 呼吸	appetite〔'æpə,taɪt〕*n.* 食欲
indigestion〔,ɪndaɪ'dʒɛstʃən〕*n.* 消化不良	
nauseate〔'nɔzɪ,et〕*v.* 使作嘔	vomit〔'vɑmɪt〕*v.* 嘔吐
feel sick 想吐；噁心	stomach〔'stʌmək〕*n.* 胃
heartburn〔'hɑrt,bɝn〕*n.* 心痛	upset〔ʌp'sɛt〕*adj.* 難過的
persistent〔pɚ'sɪstənt〕*adj.* 不斷的	abdomen〔'æbdəmən〕*n.* 腹部
diarrhea〔,daɪə'riə〕*n.* 腹瀉	loose bowels 拉肚子
swollen〔'swolən〕*adj.* 腫脹的	constipate〔'kɑnstə,pet〕*v.* 使便秘
sprain〔spren〕*v.* 扭傷	ankle〔'æŋkl̩〕*n.* 腳踝

●—— 生病了 ——●

♤ I'm feeling sick.　　　　　　　我想吐。

♤ I'm not feeling well.　　　　　我覺得不舒服。

♤ I'm **under the weather**.　　　我身體不舒服。

♧ I feel *faint*.　　　　　　　　　　　我覺得暈眩。

♧ I get tired easily.　　　　　　　　　我很容易累。

♧ I feel I'm *in a daze*.　　　　　　　我覺得頭昏眼花。

♧ I'm having my *period*. I've　　　　我今天生理期到了，肚子很
got *cramps*, and I don't feel　　　痛，什麼事都不想做。
like doing anything today.

♧ I have a *fever*.　　　　　　　　　　我發燒。

♧ I have a *slight* fever.　　　　　　　我有點發燒。

♧ I've been *feverish* since last　　　我從昨晚就開始發燒。
night.

♧ I have a *sharp pain*.　　　　　　　我痛得很厲害。

♧ I have a *dull* pain.　　　　　　　　我覺得隱隱作痛。

♧ I have a *throbbing* pain.　　　　　我覺得陣陣劇痛。

♧ I feel cold.　　　　　　　　　　　　我覺得冷。

♧ I have a *chill*.　　　　　　　　　　我感到一陣寒慄。

♧ I've caught a cold and it's　　　　我感冒愈來愈嚴重。
getting worse.

♧ I have *a running nose*.　　　　　　我流鼻水。

♤ My nose keeps *bleed*ing. 　　　　我一直流鼻血。

♤ My nose is stopped up. 　　　　　我鼻塞。

♤ I have a *stuffy nose*. 　　　　　我鼻塞。

♤ I'm *uncomfortable* because 　　我鼻子不通，覺得很不舒服。
my nose is stuffed up.

♤ I *sneeze* all the time. 　　　　我一直在打噴嚏。

♤ I *cough* a lot. 　　　　　　　　我咳得很厲害。

♤ I can't stop coughing. 　　　　　我無法不咳嗽。

♤ My throat is full of *phlegm*. 　我的喉嚨有很多痰。

♤ I have a *headache*. 　　　　　　我頭痛。

♤ My head feels heavy. 　　　　　　我覺得頭很沈重。

♤ I have a throbbing headache. 　我覺得陣陣頭痛。

♤ I have a *sore throat*. 　　　　　我喉嚨痛。

♤ It *hurts* when I *swallow*. 　　我吞食時很痛。

♤ I have a pain in my chest. 　　我的胸部很痛。

---

swallow〔'swɑlo〕*v.* 吞　　chest〔tʃɛst〕*n.* 胸

♤ My heart **palpitates**.
我的心卜卜地跳。

♤ I sometimes have severe **palpitations**.
我有時心跳得很快。

♤ I can't catch my **breath**.
我呼吸困難。

♤ I have a poor **appetite**.
我食欲不振。

♤ I don't have any appetite.
我沒有食欲。

♤ I have **indigestion**.
我消化不良。

♤ I'm **nauseated**.
我覺得反胃。

♤ I feel like **vomit**ing.
我想吐。

♤ I **feel sick** to my **stomach**.
我覺得噁心。

♤ I've got **heartburn**.
我心痛。

♤ I have an **upset** stomach.
我胃不舒服。

♤ I feel a sharp pain in my stomach.
我胃疼得很厲害。

♤ I feel a slight but **persistent** pain in my **abdomen**.
我覺得肚子不斷地微微作痛。

♤ I have **diarrhea**.
我拉肚子。

♤ I have **loose bowels**.
我拉肚子。

♤ My abdomen feels **swollen**.
我覺得肚子發脹。

♤ I've been **constipated** for three days.
我便秘三天了。

♤ I fell down and broke my right arm.
我跌倒，右手臂骨折了。

♤ I **sprained** my **ankle**.
我扭傷了脚踝。

Feeling Sick ....

A : ***I have no appetite.*** 我沒胃口。

B : What do you think it is？你覺得是什麼原因呢？

A : I don't know. I think I should see a doctor.
我不知道，我想我該去看醫生。

B : I'll call the doctor to make an appointment.
我會打電話給醫生約個時間。

*   *   *

A : ***I have a terrible headache today.*** 我今天頭痛得很厲害。

B : You've been too busy lately. You need a rest.
你最近太忙了，需要休息一下。

A : Do you really think so？你真的這麼認為嗎？

B : I know so. Take it easy for a while and your headache will
be gone. 是的。放輕鬆一下，頭痛就會消失了。

---

terrible〔ˈtɛrəbḷ〕*adj.* 劇烈的

咳嗽時，用食指用力壓兩個
耳垂下面的部分，這樣可以
減少喉頭附近的黏膜刺激，
而能減輕或是停止咳嗽。

Warm-up

medical 〔'mɛdɪkl̩〕 *adj.* 內科的

medical examination 體檢   check 〔tʃɛk〕 *v.* 檢查

pharmacy 〔'fɑrməsɪ〕 *n.* 藥房   fill 〔fɪl〕 *v.* 配（藥方）

prescription 〔prɪ'skrɪpʃən〕 *n.* 藥方

prescribe 〔prɪ'skraɪb〕 *v.* 開藥方

painkiller 〔'pen,kɪlɚ〕 *n.* 止痛藥

diagnosis 〔,daɪəg'nosɪs〕 *n.* 診斷

available 〔ə'veləbl̩〕 *adj.* 可得的；在的

● 找醫生 ●

♤ I'd like to see the doctor.　　　　　我想去看醫生。

♤ I'd like to have a *medical*　　　　我想去做體檢。
examination.

♤ I want to have my heart　　　　　　我想找醫生檢查我的心臟。
*check*ed by a doctor.

♤ Where can I find a *pharmacy*　　　這附近哪裏有藥房？
around here ?

♤ Do you have any good medicine　　你有沒有治頭痛的特效藥？
for a headache ?

♤ Will you *fill* this *prescription,* please?　請你照這藥方配藥好嗎？

♤ Would you *prescribe* a *painkiller,*　請你開一劑止痛藥好嗎？
please ?

♤ What is your *diagnosis* ?　　　　　你的診斷結果如何？

Seeing a Doctor ··

A : ***Would you prescribe a painkiller, please*** ?
   請你開一劑止痛藥好嗎？

B : All right. Bring this prescription to the drugstore and
   have it filled.
   好的，你帶著這藥方到藥房去配藥。

＊　　　　＊　　　　＊

A : ***I'd like to see the doctor.*** What time will be convenient?
   我想去看醫生，何時方便？

B : Let me see … The doctor will be available at 10 o'clock
   this Friday. How does that suit you?
   我看看…醫生這星期五上午十點會在，這個時間可以嗎？

A : That's fine with me. 我可以。

---

suit 〔sut〕 *v.* 適合

家庭小常識　洋葱對胃病患者不利，但用洋葱粉攪拌成糊，塗於胸部，却能治支氣管炎及呼吸系統的疾病。

Warm-up

aspirin〔'æspərɪn〕*n.* 阿斯匹靈
pale〔pel〕*adj.* 蒼白的　　　　bowel〔'baʊəl〕*n.* 腸
movement〔'muvmənt〕*n.* 通便；大便
bone〔bon〕*n.* 骨骼　　　　give up 放棄
temperature〔'tɛmprətʃə〕*n.* 體溫
take one's temperature 量體溫　awful〔'ɔfl〕*adj.* 極不舒服的

● 照顧病人 ●

♤ Take this *aspirin* now.　　　　現在吃下這顆阿斯匹靈。

♤ Do you have a cold?　　　　你感冒了嗎？

♤ Do you have a sore throat?　　你喉嚨痛嗎？

♤ Do you have a fever?　　　　你發燒了嗎？

♤ What's the matter?　　　　怎麼了？

♤ You must have caught a cold.　你一定是感冒了。

♤ Open your mouth wide.　　　嘴巴張大一點。

♤ Is there anything wrong?　　哪裏不舒服嗎？

♤ You really ought to see a　　你真的應該再去看醫生。
doctor again.

＊＊

wide〔waɪd〕*adv.* 大大地

♤ You look *pale.*   你臉色很蒼白。

♤ Do you have *bowel movements regularly* ?   你有沒有按時上大號？

♤ Did you have movements this morning ?   你今天早上上過大號了沒？

♤ Does it hurt ?   會痛嗎？

♤ Where is the *pain* ?   哪裏會痛？

♤ Does it hurt when I touch it?   我碰到那裏會痛嗎？

♤ Do you have any difficulty because of the pain ?   疼痛有沒有帶給你任何不便?

♤ It's good that there were no *bones* broken.   幸好骨頭沒斷。

♤ I'm afraid you'll have to *give up* hockey for several weeks.   你恐怕好幾個禮拜不能打曲棍球。

**———————————————

     touch 〔tʌtʃ〕 *v.* 碰觸
     hockey 〔'hɑkɪ〕 *n.* 曲棍球

Attending to the Sick ·······················

A : **What's the matter? Do you have a cold?**
　　怎麼回事？你感冒了嗎？

B : I don't feel so good. I think it's a fever.
　　我人不太舒服，大概是發燒了吧。

A : Here, I'll take your temperature.
　　來這裏，讓我量量看你的體溫。

　　　　　　＊　　　　　　＊　　　　　　＊

A : How do you feel? 你覺得如何？

B : I feel awful. 我覺得很不舒服。

A : **You really ought to see a doctor again.**
　　你真應該再去看醫生。

B : You're right. Do you know the name of a good doctor?
　　沒錯。你有沒有認識什麼好醫生？

家庭小常識　醋的妙用實在不少，你或許不知道，跌倒腫痛凝血時，用棉花沾一些醋，細揉患處，能消腫散血呢！

Unit 13

Small Talk 閒話家常

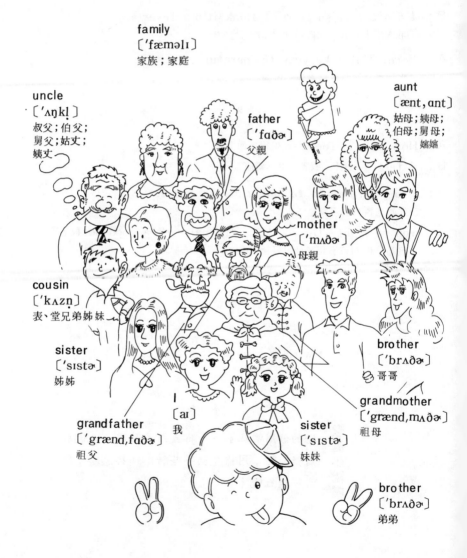

family
〔'fæməlɪ〕
家族；家庭

uncle
〔'ʌŋkl̩〕
叔父；伯父；
舅父；姑丈；
姨丈

father
〔'faðɚ〕
父親

aunt
〔ænt, ɑnt〕
姑母；姨母；
伯母；舅母；
嬸嬸

mother
〔'mʌðɚ〕
母親

cousin
〔'kʌzn̩〕
表、堂兄弟姊妹

sister
〔'sɪstɚ〕
姊姊

I
〔aɪ〕
我

brother
〔'brʌðɚ〕
哥哥

grandmother
〔'grænd,mʌðɚ〕
祖母

grandfather
〔'grænd,faðɚ〕
祖父

sister
〔'sɪstɚ〕
妹妹

brother
〔'brʌðɚ〕
弟弟

Warm-up

satisfied 〔'sætɪs,faɪd〕 *adj.* 滿意的

refusal 〔rɪ'fjuzl̩〕 *n.* 拒絕   dumbfound 〔,dʌm'faʊnd〕*v.* 使驚愕

embarrassment 〔ɪm'bærəsmənt〕 *n.* 妨害

depressed 〔dɪ'prɛst〕 *adj.* 沮喪的

fire 〔faɪr〕 *v.* 解雇   union 〔'junjən〕 *n.* 工會

quit 〔kwɪt〕 *v.* 辭職   at work 進行中；在工作中

factory 〔'fæktrɪ, -tərɪ〕 *n.* 工廠

finish 〔'fɪnɪʃ〕 *v.* 完成   on time 準時

meeting 〔'mitɪŋ〕 *n.* 會議   resign 〔rɪ'zaɪn〕 *v.* 辭職

boss 〔bɔs〕 *n.* 老板   tell sb. off 斥責

upset 〔ʌp'sɛt〕 *adj.* 煩亂的   stress 〔strɛs〕 *n.* 壓力

on the blink 不健康   reception 〔rɪ'sɛpʃən〕 *n.* 應接；接待

get blamed 受到譴責   manager 〔'mænɪdʒɚ〕 *n.* 經理

make up one's mind 下定決心   work overtime 加班

enter 〔'ɛntɚ〕 *v.* 加入   career field 行業；工作領域

yell at sb. 破口罵人   be fed up with 受夠了；感到厭煩

● 工 作 ●

♤ I'm not ***satisfied*** with my job.　　我不太滿意自己的工作。

♤ Her ***refusal*** to do the job left me ***dumbfounded***.　　她拒絕做那工作，使我十分驚訝。

♤ He was an ***embarrassment*** to the company.　　他是公司的害群之馬。

♤ I'm really ***depressed*** about my job.　　我的工作令我十分沮喪。

♤ I'm sorry to hear about your being *fired*.

聽到你被解雇，我十分難過。

♤ I'm sorry to hear about the trouble with *the union*.

聽到工會所面臨的麻煩，我很遺憾。

♤ I was surprised to hear about your planning to *quit*.

聽說你想辭職，我覺得十分驚訝。

♤ How are things *at work*?

工作還順利嗎？

♤ How are things at the *factory*?

工廠經營得如何？

♤ How do you like your new job?

你覺得那份新工作如何呢？

♤ I didn't *finish* the job *on time*.

我沒準時完成工作。

♤ How did the *meeting* go?

會議進行得如何？

♤ Are you serious about *resigning*?

你真的要辭職嗎？

♤ The *boss* just *told* me *off* over the phone. I have no idea what he's so *upset* about.

老板剛才在電話中罵了我一頓，真不知道他為什麼這麼生氣。

♤ They always give me things to do at the last minute.

他們總是在下班前一刻給我一堆事情做。

---

serious〔'sɪrɪəs〕*adj.* 認真的

♧ It's always "Bring us tea" and "Make copies"—they never even say "please." What do they think we are?"

他們總是命令道「幫我們倒茶」「複寫幾份」，從不說聲「請」，他們把我們當成什麼了？

♤ The *stress* just keeps building up. My stomach's been bothering me lately.

壓力愈來愈重，害得最近我的胃一直不舒服。

♧ You're lucky if it's just your stomach. My liver's *on the blink* because of all the *receptions* I've been going to.

如果只是胃不舒服，那你很幸運。所有的應酬喝酒，危害了我的肝臟。

♤ Why do I *get blamed*? It was the *manager*'s mistake.

爲何我被罵？那是經理的錯。

♧ Is he saying I should finish this by next week? It'll kill me!

他是不是說我下星期結束前要做完？那會要了我的命！

♧ I *made up my mind* not to *work overtime* today, and this happens...

我已決定今天不加班，但發生了…

**

liver ['lɪvə] *n.* 肝臟

Work ···

A: **I'm not satisfied with my job.** 我不太滿意我的工作。

B: What about entering another career field?
何不轉行呢？

A: But I need training to do that. 但是轉行需要接受訓練。

B: There are some night school courses you can take.
你可以修些夜校的課。

A: That's a good idea. I'll call their office today.
這主意不錯，我今天就打電話到他們的辦事處問。

＊　　　　　＊　　　　　＊

A: **I didn't finish the job on time.** 我沒準時做完工作。

B: Did the boss yell at you? 老板有沒有對你破口大罵？

A: No, it's a good thing he's on vacation this week.
沒有，還好這星期他渡假去了。

＊　　　　　＊　　　　　＊

A: **Are you serious about resigning?**
你眞的要辭職嗎？

B: Sure. I'm fed up with the boss.
當然，我實在受夠了我們老板。

A: What will you do after you resign?
辭職後你有何打算？

B: A manager at another company wants to give me a job.
另一家公司的經理答應給我一份工作做。

Warm-up

French 〔frɛntʃ〕 *n.* 法文
test 〔tɛst〕 *n.* 考試
make it 成功；達成
team 〔tim〕 *n.* 隊伍

pass 〔pæs, pɑs〕 *v.* 通過；合格
algebra 〔ˈældʒəbrə〕 *n.* 代數
track 〔træk〕 *n.* 田徑賽

──────●學　校●──────

♤ Why don't you study *French* instead?

你爲何不改唸法文呢？

♤ How was school today?

今天在學校怎麼樣呢？

♤ I think you should tell your teacher about it.

我覺得你該告訴老師這件事。

♤ How is your new teacher?

你的新老師如何？

♤ Is it true that you *pas*sed the test?

你真的通過考試了？

♤ How can you just watch TV when you have a *test* tomorrow?

明天要考試了，你怎麼還在看電視？

♤ Don't tell me that you don't want to take *algebra*.

不要告訴我說你不想修代數。

♤ Do you think you'll *make it* on the school *track team*?

你真的認爲自己可以參加學校的田徑隊嗎？

♤ You can ride your bike to school or take the bus.

你可以騎腳踏車或搭公車上學。

Schools ···

A： Algebra is so boring. 代數眞是無聊。

B： ***Why don't you study French instead***？
那你何不改唸法文呢？

A： But French is boring too.
可是法文也是一樣無聊。

B： I guess you just can't please some people.
我想有些人總是很難取悅的。

＊　　　　　＊　　　　　＊

A： ***How is your new teacher***？ 你的新老師如何？

B： He's boring. I almost fell asleep in class today.
他很無聊，今天上課我差點睡著了。

A： Do you have any good teachers？
你有不錯的老師嗎？

B： Well, Ms. Andersen is OK. She tells a lot of jokes.
嗯，安德森女士還好，她會說很多笑話。

小學	中學	高中
elementary school	junior high school	senior high school

Warm-up

watch out 小心;注意   in a foul / bad mood 心情不好
cheer sb. up 使某人高興

──────●家　人●──────

♤ Hi! Mom, I'm home.　　　　　　　嗨！媽，我回來了！

♤ Better watch out. Dad's in a　　你最好小心，爸爸心情不好。
foul mood.

♤ I've finished my homework.　　　我的功課做完了。

♤ Can I go out with my friends?　我可以和朋友出去嗎？

♤ Dad's out. Let's go play.　　　　爸爸不在，我們來玩吧！

♤ You had better clean up. Mom's　你最好打掃一下，媽快回來
going to be home soon.　　　　　了。

♤ It's your turn to mow the lawn　今天該你割草坪的草了。
today.

♤ Dad said you can't watch TV　　爸爸說除非你功課做完，否
unless you finish your homework.　則不准看電視。

♤ Be back in time for dinner,　　親愛的，要回來吃晚飯喔！
dear.

＊＊───────────────

mow〔mo〕 *v.* 割（草）　　lawn〔lɔn〕 *n.* 草坪

The Family ....

A : ***Better watch out！ Dad's in a bad mood today.***
　　你最好小心，爸爸今天心情不好。

B : What happened？ Did he have a fight with Mom？
　　怎麼了？他和媽吵架了嗎？

A : No, I think he had a bad day at work.
　　沒有，我想是他工作上的不愉快。

B : Poor Dad！ Let's go cheer him up.
　　可憐的爸爸，我們去讓他開心一下吧！

　　　　　　*　　　　　　　*　　　　　　　*

A : ***Can I go out with my friends***, Mom？ 媽，我可以和朋友出去嗎？

B : Not before you finish mowing the lawn. It's your turn
　　today, remember？
　　你還沒割完草坪的草之前不可以出去。今天該你了，記得嗎？

A : Aw shucks！ I promise to do it tomorrow. Can I go, please？
　　哎呀，糟糕！我發誓我明天一定去做。我可以去嗎？拜託！

B : Alright, dear, but be back in time for dinner.
　　好吧！親愛的，不過要回來吃晚飯喔！

　　　　　　*　　　　　　　*　　　　　　　*

A : Dad's out. Let's put on the TV. 爸爸不在，我們來開電視吧！

B : No, ***Dad said you can't watch TV unless you finish your
　　homework.*** 不行，爸爸說除非你功課做完，否則不准看電視。

A : But he wouldn't know, he's not at home.
　　但是他不會知道的，他又不在家。

B : Yes he would because I'll tell him.
　　他會知道，因為我會告訴他。

Warm-up

be serious about sb. 對某人認眞

treat〔trit〕v. 對待　　　　be dying to 渴望

look forward to 期待　　　type〔taɪp〕n. 型

be interested in sb. 對某人有興趣

————● 朋　友 ●————

♧ *Are* you *serious about* Catherine?

你對凱瑟琳是很認眞的嗎？

♧ Do you want to go fishing with us tomorrow?

你明天要不要和我們一起去釣魚？

♧ You must be Cindy's friend.

你一定是辛蒂的朋友。

♧ I was surprised by the news that he won't come.

聽到他不會來的消息，使我很驚訝。

♧ I shouldn't have *treat*ed her so badly.

我當初不該對她這麼壞。

♧ I'm *dying to* hear all about your trip.

我很想知道你旅行的詳細情形。

♤ I'm *looking forward to* meeting your mother.

我很想見你的母親。

♤ Karen, this is Joan, a good friend of mine.

凱倫，這是瓊，她是我的好朋友。

♤ I'm pleased to meet you.

很高興認識你。

♤ I've heard so much about you from Bill.

我常聽比爾提起你。

♤ Wow! He's really my *type*!

哇！他就是我喜歡的那一型！

♤ I wonder if he really is interested in her.

我懷疑他是否眞的對她有興趣。

♤ Charlie, I'd like you to meet my friend Kate.

查理，我跟你介紹我的朋友凱特。

♤ Yes, I know Bill. He's an old friend from back in college.

嗯，我認識比爾，他是大學時代的老朋友。

♤ Any friend of Joe's is a friend of mine.

喬的朋友就是我的朋友。

♤ She's an old friend that I haven't seen for years.

她是我多年沒見面的老朋友。

Friends ···

A : **Do you want to go fishing with us tomorrow?**
你明天要和我們一起去釣魚嗎？

B : Well, I already have something planned.
哦，我已經有別的計劃了。

A : What about next weekend？那下個禮拜呢？

B : No problem. Make it next weekend.
沒問題，下個禮拜就可以。

＊　　　　　＊　　　　　＊

A : **I'm dying to hear all about your trip.**
我很想聽聽你旅行的事。

B : Well, it was OK. It wasn't the best vacation I've had.
嗯，還好啦。但這次沒有以前的好玩。

A : I still want to hear about it.
我還是想聽你說。

 好友生日，送份禮物表達心意，增進友誼，
但可千萬別送鐘（終）！

Warm-up

rain〔ren〕v. 下雨　　　　　windy〔'wɪndɪ〕adj. 颱風的
monsoon〔mɑn'sun〕n. 季風　　humid〔'hjumɪd〕adj. 潮濕的
It rains cats and dogs. 大雨傾盆。
fog〔fɑg, fɔg〕n. 霧　　　　freezing〔'frizɪŋ〕adj. 寒冷的
cloudburst〔'klaʊd,bɝst〕n. 驟雨
warm〔wɔrm〕adj. 暖和的　　　they said… 據說～

● 天　氣 ●

♤ Is it going to **rain** today？　　　今天會下雨嗎？

♤ Do you think it will be
windy today？　　　　　　　你覺得今天會颱風嗎？

♤ Winter will be arriving late
this year.　　　　　　　　　今年的冬天會來得比較遲。

♤ We're going to have a very
hot summer.　　　　　　　　今年的夏天會很熱。

♤ It's **monsoon** season now.　　現在是吹季風的季節。

♧ It's hot and *humid* in July.　　七月既熱且潮濕。

♧ It's *raining cats and dogs*.　　大雨傾盆。

♧ The fog is so thick you can cut it with a knife.　　霧濃得就像可以用刀子劃開一樣。

♧ It's *freezing* outside!　　外面真冷！

♧ We usually have an afternoon *cloudburst* this time of year.　　每年的這個時候，午後通常會有驟雨。

♧ Will it be *warm* this weekend?　　這個週末會很暖和嗎？

♧ *They said* it will rain tomorrow.　　據說明天會下雨。

♧ It's foggy in the morning this time of year.　　每年的這個時候，早上通常有霧。

♧ You couldn't ask for a better day.　　天氣再好不過了。

家庭小常識　你知道憑飛機後面噴出的煙雲凝結尾，可以預測天氣嗎？凡凝結尾很快消失，表示天氣乾燥，未來幾天的天氣一定晴朗；若凝結尾久久不消失，反而變粗變長，則表示空氣中的濕氣很重，陰雨天即將來臨。

Weather ··

A： It sure has been hot and humid this month.
　　這個月的確又熱又潮濕。

B： ***It's monsoon season now.*** 現在是吹季風的季節。

A： How long will monsoon season last？
　　這樣的季節會持續多久呢？

B： About three or four months. 大概三或四個月吧。

　　　　　　　　＊　　　　　　＊　　　　　　＊

A： ***It's raining cats and dogs.*** 雨下得眞大。

B： We usually have an afternoon cloudburst this time of year.
　　每年的這個時候，午後通常會有驟雨。

A： Maybe I should buy an umbrella. 也許我該買把傘。

B： A good raincoat is also nice to have.
　　買件好的雨衣也很不錯。

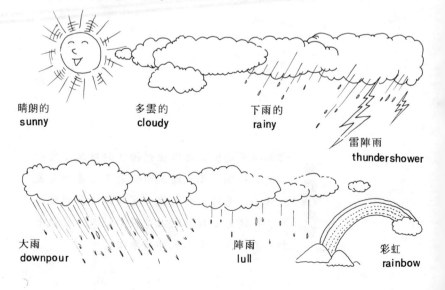

晴朗的
sunny

多雲的
cloudy

下雨的
rainy

雷陣雨
thundershower

大雨
downpour

陣雨
lull

彩虹
rainbow

Warm-up

What time do you have？現在幾點了？
What a relief！鬆了口氣！ definitely〔'dɛfənɪtlɪ〕*adv.* 的確
call it a day 今天到此為止

● 時 間 ●

♤ What's the best time for fishing？ 何時去釣魚最適當？

♤ When does the baseball game start？ 棒球賽何時開始？

♤ My first class is at eight thirty. 我第一節課是在八點半上。

♤ The bus takes half an hour to get to school. 搭那輛公車上學要半個小時。

♤ ***What time do you have***？ My watch has stopped. 現在幾點？我的錶停了。

♤ When will you get up tomorrow？ 明天你何時會起床？

♤ How often do you have to work overtime？ 你多久加班一次？

♤ Is it time to go yet？ 現在可以走了嗎？

♤ ***What a relief***！ It's finally time to go. 鬆了一口氣，總算可以走了！

♤ It's ***definitely*** getting late. I should ***call it a day***. 的確愈來愈晚了，我今天應該就做到這裡。

Time ···

A : **When does the baseball game start ?**
　　棒球賽何時開始？

B : Seven thirty, I think. 大概是七點半吧。

A : In that case I've got enough time to buy some popcorn.
　　這樣的話，我就有時間去買些爆米花來吃。

B : You're a real couch potato, you know that？
　　你知道嗎？你真是個愛看電視的懶骨頭。

　　　　　　　＊　　　　　＊　　　　　＊

A : When do you have to be at school in the morning？
　　你早上必須何時到校？

B : **My first class is at eight thirty.**
　　我第一節課是在八點半上。

A : You have to get up early then.
　　那你就得早點起床。

B : I get up at six thirty. 我通常六點半起床。

──────────────

couch potato （俚語，指成天坐在沙發上看電視的）懶骨頭

Warm-up

first run 首輪；首映（電影）
performance〔pə'fɔrməns〕*n.* 演出
credit card 信用卡   offer〔'ɔfə, 'ɑfə〕*v.* 提供
discount〔'dɪskaʊnt〕*n.* 折扣   sell out 售完
row〔ro〕*n.* 排   balcony〔'bælkənɪ〕*n.* 戲院包廂
balcony seat 包廂座位   in advance 事先
concert〔'kɑnsɜt〕*n.* 音樂會   act〔ækt〕*n.* 一幕

———● 觀賞表演 ●———

♤ Is it *a first run* movie?   這部是首輪影片嗎？

♤ When's the next *performance*?   下次的演出是什麼時候？

♤ Has the play started?   戲開演了嗎？

♤ Use my credit card to pay for   用我的信用卡買票。
   the ticket.

♤ Do they *offer* student *discounts*?   有學生優待票嗎？

♤ Is the performance *sold out*?   那場表演的票全部售完了嗎？

♤ Buy two seats in *row* nine.   買兩張第九排的票。

♤ Do they have any *balcony seats* left?   他們還有包廂的座位嗎？

♤ Can we buy tickets *in advance*?   能事先買票嗎？

♤ How was the *concert* last night?   昨晚的音樂會如何？

♤ How long is the play?   這場戲多長？

♤ I'm afraid that the performance   恐怕那場表演的票早就賣完
   is already sold out.   了。

Going to the Show··

A： ***Has the play started***? 戲開演了嗎？

B： Not yet. We have to hurry or they won't let us in.
　　還沒。我們必須快點，否則他們就不讓我們進去了。

A： What if we're late？ 如果遲到怎麼辦？

B： Then we have to wait until the second act.
　　那就得等下一幕了。

＊　　　　　＊　　　　　＊

A： ***Is it a first run movie***？ 這是首輪電影嗎？

B： It sure is. That's why it's so hard to get tickets.
　　當然是，所以票才這麼難買。

A： Can we buy tickets in advance？
　　可以事先買票嗎？

B： No, not at this movie theater.
　　不行，這家戲院不賣預售票。

Warm-up

drive-in 〔'draɪv,ɪn〕 *adj*。免下車的

traffic 〔'træfɪk〕 *n.* 交通　　drive-thru 免下車供餐服務

race track 賽車道；跑道　　speed limit 時速限制

flow 〔flo〕 *n.* 流動　　gas 〔gæs〕 *n.* 汽油

empty 〔'ɛmptɪ〕 *adj.* 空的　　jam 〔dʒæm〕 *n.* 擁擠

tire 〔taɪr〕 *n.* 輪胎　　engine 〔'ɛndʒən〕 *n.* 引擎

flat 〔flæt〕 *adj.* (輪胎) 洩了氣的

freeway 〔'fri,we〕 *n.* 高速公路

pull over　把車停在路邊　　light 〔laɪt〕 *adj.* 輕微的

stop-and-go　停停走走的　　parking spot 停車位

---●　在車內　●---

♤ Let's go to a ***drive-in*** movie.　　我們去看一部免下車的電影吧。

♤ The ***traffic*** sure is awful this time of day.　　每天這時候交通一定非常擁擠。

♤ Too bad this car doesn't fly.　　這部車不能飛，真是太可惜了。

♤ Don't eat in the car.　　別在車上吃東西。

♤ Does that fast-food restaurant have a ***drive-thru*** ?　　這家速食店有免下車供餐服務嗎？

♤ Slow down! This isn't a ***race track***.　　開慢一點，這裏不是賽車道!

♤ Does this car have a radio ?　　這部車有收音機嗎？

♤ Good thing this car has air conditioning.

這部車有冷氣眞好！

♤ The *speed limit* is 60 km per hour here.

這裏的時速限制是六十公里。

♤ I'm just going with the *flow* of traffic.

我只是隨著川流不息的車陣往前移動。

♤ My car might not have enough *gas*, it's almost *empty*.

我的車子汽油也許不夠，快用光了。

♤ With this traffic *jam*, I think I'll be late for work.

交通這麼擁塞，我想我上班要遲到了。

♤ I think one of my *tires* is going *flat*.

我看我的一個車胎快爆了。

♤ There is something wrong with the *engine*.

引擎出了點毛病。

♤ I'll turn onto the *freeway*.

我要開上高速公路。

♤ I got *pulled over* by a police car.

我被一輛警車攔截下來。

♤ I hope the traffic will be *light* today.

我希望今天交通順暢一點。

♤ I hate *stop-and-go* driving.

我討厭交通擁擠時停停走走地開車。

♤ Is there a *parking spot* around here?

這附近有停車的地方嗎？

Inside the Car ···

A : My goodness! The traffic sure is awful this time of day.
　　我的天！每天的這個時候交通眞是糟透了！

B : You bet! And the hot weather only makes things worse.
　　對啊！而且這麼熱的天氣使情況更糟。

A : ***Good thing this car has air conditioning.*** I would actually
　　die if it didn't.
　　幸好這部車有冷氣。如果沒有，我簡直會熱死。

＊　　　　＊　　　　＊

A : Aren't you driving too fast?
　　你是不是開得太快了？

B : No, I'm not. ***The speed limit is 60 km per hour here.***
　　不會的，這裏的時速限制是六十公里。

家庭小常識　　會暈車、暈船的朋友，外出旅行時，上船或登車之前，切記不要吃甜食哦！這樣可以防止暈眩。

Warm-up

wander 〔'wɑndɚ〕 *v.* 無目的地各處行走

set up 搭（帳篷）   tent 〔tɛnt〕 *n.* 帳篷

firewood 〔'faɪr,wʊd〕 *n.* 柴   fetch 〔fɛtʃ〕 *v.* 取來

make a fire 升火   flashlight 〔'flæʃ,laɪt〕*n.*手電筒

get lost 迷路   battery 〔'bætərɪ〕 *n.* 電池

● 露　營 ●

♤ Be careful not to ***wander*** too far.　　小心點，別逛得太遠了。

♤ Do you need help ***setting up*** the ***tent***?　　要不要我幫忙搭帳篷？

♤ Can you look for some ***firewood***?　　能不能找些柴來？

♤ Can you ***fetch*** some water?　　去拿些水來好嗎？

♤ Can you ***make a fire***?　　能不能升個火？

♤ Make sure the fire is out.　　要確定火已完全熄滅了。

♤ Did you bring a ***flashlight***?　　你有帶手電筒來嗎？

♤ Let's go get some firewood.　　我們去撿些柴吧！

Camping ···

A : **Be careful not to wander too far.**
　　小心，別走太遠了。

B : I know my way around these woods.
　　這森林附近的路我都很熟。

A : It's going to be dark soon. You might get lost.
　　再過不久就要天黑了，你會迷路的。

B : OK, I won't go very far. 好吧，我不會走太遠的。

＊　　　　　＊　　　　　＊

A : **Did you bring a flashlight**? 你帶手電筒了嗎？

B : Of course I did. 當然帶了。

A : What about batteries? 那電池呢？

B : I brought batteries too. Do you think I forgot?
　　也帶了。你想我可能會忘嗎？

A : I'm just making sure. 我只是想確定一下罷了。

營火
campfire

營區
campsite

Warm-up

tennis 〔ˈtɛnɪs〕 *n.* 網球	doubles 〔ˈdʌblz〕 *n. pl.* 雙打
partner 〔ˈpɑrtnɚ〕 *n.* 搭檔	toss 〔tɔs〕 *v.* 猜拳
service 〔ˈsɝvɪs〕 *n.* 發球	serve 〔sɝv〕 *v.* 發球
score 〔skor, skɔr〕 *n.* 比數	tie 〔taɪ〕 *v.* 不分勝負

putt 〔pʌt〕 *v.* (高爾夫球) 以球棍輕擊使球入洞

birdie 〔ˈbɝdɪ〕 *n.* (高爾夫球) 比標準桿少一桿入洞

iron 〔ˈaɪɚn〕 *n.* (高爾夫球) 球桿　　shot 〔ʃɑt〕 *n.* 擊球

bunker 〔ˈbʌŋkɚ〕 *n.* 高爾夫球場上人工的障礙沙洞

caddie 〔ˈkædɪ〕 *n.* 球僮	green 〔grin〕 *n.* 果嶺

ping-pong 〔ˈpɪŋ,pɑŋ, -,pɔŋ〕 *n.* 乒乓球

windsurfing 〔ˈwɪnd,sɝfɪŋ〕 *n.* 風浪板

ski 〔ski〕 *v.* 滑雪	warm up 暖身
court 〔kort, kɔrt〕 *n.* 場地	super 〔ˈsupɚ〕 *adj.* 漂亮的
drive 〔draɪv〕 *v.* 發(投)球	root for 為～加油
pitcher 〔ˈpɪtʃɚ〕 *n.* 投手	strike sb. out 將某人三振出局

ball and strike count 球數

tournament 〔ˈtɝnəmənt, ˈtʊr-〕 *n.* 比賽

● 運　動 ●

♤ What sports do you like?　　　你喜歡什麼運動?

♤ What sports do you play?　　　你做什麼運動?

♤ Where can we play *tennis*?　　我們能去哪裏打網球呢?

♤ I want you to be my *doubles partner*.　　我想要請你當我雙打的搭檔。

♤ Let's *toss* for *service*.　　　猜拳看誰先發球。

游泳
swimming

滑雪
skiing

溜冰
skating

♤ What's the *score*?　現在比數是多少?

♤ The game is *tied*.　比賽平手。

♤ Oh no, I three *putted* again.　噢!糟糕!我又打了三桿球才進洞。

♤ You've got a chance for a *birdie*.　你有機會比標準桿少一桿入洞。

♤ Use a seven *iron* for this *shot*.　用七號球桿打。

♤ I can't get the ball out of the *bunker*.　我無法把球從沙洞裏取出來。

♤ Who's winning?　現在誰領先?

♤ I'm getting better at *ping-pong*.　我乒乓球打得越來越好了。

♤ *Windsurfing* is fun once you know how to do it.　如果知道如何控制的話,風浪板是十分好玩的活動。

♤ We're *going skiing* this weekend. Want to join us?　我們這個週末要去滑雪,你要一起去嗎?

♤ You're so good. 你球打得真好。

♤ Let's practice a little to *warm up*. 我們做一下暖身的練習。

♤ You *serve* first. 你先發球。

♤ I'll take the *court*. 我選場地。

♤ That was a *super* shot. 真是漂亮的一擊。

♤ I'm good at *driving*. 我擅於發（投）球。

♤ Let's take five. 我們休息五分鐘吧！

♤ Which team are you *rooting for*? 你在為哪一隊加油？

♤ This *pitcher*'s got a good fast ball. 投手擲了一個快速直球。

♤ The pitcher *struck* him *out*. 投手將他三振出局。

♤ What's the *ball and strike count*? 現在球數是多少？

桌球
table tennis

網球
tennis

籃球
basketball

排球
volleyball

棒球
baseball

Sports ··

A : **What's the score**? 現在的比數如何？

B : The game is tied. 比賽不分勝負。

A : Who's playing? 是哪兩隊在比呢？

B : The Tigers and the Lions. 是虎隊和獅隊。

＊　　　　　＊　　　　　＊

A : Hey caddie! How far is it to the green?
嗨，球僮！這裏離果嶺還有多遠？

B : 150 yards, sir. **You can use a seven iron for this shot**.
還有一百五十碼，先生。你可以用七號球桿打。

＊　　　　　＊　　　　　＊

A : Did you hear that there's a tennis tournament this
weekend? 你有沒有聽說這個週末有網球錦標賽？

B : No, I didn't. 沒有。

A : **I want you to be my doubles partner**.
我想要你和我聯手打雙打。

B : No problem. I don't have anything planned for this weekend.
沒問題，我這個週末沒什麼事。

＊　　　　　＊　　　　　＊

A : What's the ball and strike count? 現在比數是多少？

B : Three and two. 兩好三壞。

-----

yard〔jɑrd〕*n.* 碼

說英文高手 ｜ 與傳統會話教材有何不同？

1. 我們學了那麼多年的英語會語，為什麼還不會說？

我們所使用的教材不對。傳統實況會話教材，如去郵局、在機場、看醫生等，勉強背下來，哪有機會使用？不使用就會忘記。等到有一天到了郵局，早就忘了你所學的。

2. 「說英文高手」這本書，和傳統的英語會話教材有何不同？

「說英文高手」這本書，以三句為一組，任何時候都可以說，可以對外國人說，也可以和中國人說，有時可自言自語說。例如：你幾乎天天都可以說：What a beautiful day it is！It's not too hot. It's not too cold. It's just right. 傳統的英語會話教材，都是以兩個人以上的對話為主，主角又是你，又是別人，當然記不下來。「說英文高手」的主角就是你，先從你天天可說的話開始。把你要說的話用英文表達出來，所以容易記下來。

3. 為什麼用「說英文高手」這本書，學了馬上就會說？

書中的教材，學起來有趣，一次說三句，不容易忘記。例如：你有很多機會可以對朋友說：Never give up. Never give in. Never say never.

4. 傳統會話教材目標不明確，一句句學，學了後面，忘了前面，一輩子記不起來。「說英文高手」目標明確，先從一次說三句開始，自我訓練以後，能夠隨時說六句以上，例如：你說的話，別人不相信，傳統會話只教你一句：I'm not kidding. 連這句話你都會忘掉。「說英文高手」教你一次說很多句：

I mean what I say.
I say what I mean.
I really mean it.

I'm not kidding you.
I'm not joking with you.
I'm telling you the truth.

你唸唸看，背這六句是不是比背一句容易呢？能夠一次說六句以上英文，你會有無比興奮的感覺，當說英文變成你的愛好的時候，你的目標就達成。

全省各大書局均售　◉ 書180元／錄音帶四卷500元

✌「**說英文高手**」為劉毅老師最新創作，是學習出版公司轟動全國的暢銷新書
已被多所學校採用為會話教材。本書適合高中及大學使用，也適合自修。

Editorial Staff

● **編著**／陳美黛

● **英文撰稿**

　Thomas Deneau · Edward C. Yulo

● **校訂**

　劉　毅 · 陳瑠琍 · 鄭明俊 · 張玉玲
　黃馨週 · 蔡琇瑩 · 謝靜芳 · 黃慧玉

● **校閱**

　Sean Carr · Tenzing Lobsang

● **版面設計**／張鳳儀 · 白雪嬌 · 周國成

● **版面構成**／周國成 · 白雪嬌

● **打字**／黃淑貞 · 蘇淑玲 · 倪秀梅 · 吳秋香

國立中央圖書館出版品預行編目資料

家庭英語 = Home English / 陳美黛編著 　　--一版--
　〔台北市〕：學習發行；
　〔台北市〕：紅螞蟻總經銷，1997〔民 86〕
　　面；公分
　ISBN 957-519-260-5（平裝）

　1. 英國語言—讀本
805.18　　　　　　　　　　　　　　　　　83007550

家庭英語

編　　著 / 陳 美 黛
發　行　所 / 學習出版有限公司　　　☎ (02) 2704-5525
郵 撥 帳 號 / 0512727-2 學習出版社帳戶
登　記　證 / 局版台業 2179 號
印　刷　所 / 裕強彩色印刷有限公司
台 北 門 市 / 台北市許昌街 10 號 2 F　　☎ (02) 2331-4060・2331-9209
台 中 門 市 / 台中市綠川東街 32 號 8 F 23 室　　☎ (04) 2223-2838
台灣總經銷 / 紅螞蟻圖書有限公司　　☎ (02) 2795-3656
美國總經銷 / Evergreen Book Store　　☎ (818) 2813622
本公司網址　www.learnbook.com.tw
電 子 郵 件　learnbook@learnbook.com.tw

售價：新台幣一百五十元正

2002 年 4 月 1 日一版五刷

ISBN 957-519-260-5